What others are saying...

Teachers:

"Carol has great insight into efficient and economical house cleaning tips. This book is easy to read and contains great tips for those in the cleaning business or anyone wishing to improve their cleaning skills."

Cheryl Palac,
Family and Consumer
Science Teacher

"Excellent guide for an individual wishing to start a cleaning business. Thorough, easy to read, practical information."

Beverly McGlamery,
Transitions Coodinator
Polaris Career Center

Librarian:

"Carol is an inspiration for those going into the cleaning business, encouraging people that they can succeed by following her practical advice and proven tips. Products are described and cleaning problems explained. This book provides a thorough coverage of the cleaning business not found in other resources!"

Karen Sigsworth
Branch Librarian Supervisor

Author:

"Finally, a housecleaning book that teaches the basic techniques. Anyone looking for a home industry has the perfect 'how to' with Klima's book...everything you need to know is spelled out!"

Mim Nagy - Author of
"The Complete Guidebook to
The Business of Tag and
Estate Sales"

Cleaning Professionals:

"Carol offers a thorough knowledge of the business in this detailed guide for anyone who wants to be a cleaning professional. I wish I had this book when I was starting out!"

Mark Grigson,
"Cleaning Mates"
Cleaning Service

"'Squeaky Clean' has practical how to cleaning methods that will save you valuable time and effort. Great job!"

Don and Sandy Schilling
Husband and wife cleaning
team

Squeaky Clean

by *Carol J. Klima*

First Edition

Homestead Press
8804 Harris Court
North Ridgeville, OH 44039

1-888-769-6335
homesteadpress@juno.com

Squeaky Clean

by CAROL J. KLIMA

PUBLISHED BY:

Homestead Press
8804 Harris Court
North Ridgeville, OH 44039

Printed in Canada
ISBN 0-9672207-4-2

Library of Congress PCN
2002109694

Acknowledgements

Appliance Coil Brush
  Dist. by GE Appliances/Parts Master™

Bon Ami® Cleanser
  Faultless Starch/Bon Ami Co.

Beeswax Wood Preserver
  Luster Products™

Bottle Brush with Lambswool Tip
  Mr. Scrubmaster® / Phoenixware®

Brasso®
  Dist. by Reckitt Benckiser, Inc.

Brillo®
  Church & Dwight Co., Inc.

Ultra Caddy
  Sterilite® Corp

Clorox Clean-Up® & Clorox bleach®
  The Clorox Co.

Comet©
  Procter & Gamble

Craftsman® Screwdriver
  Sears®

DL Permatex® Hand Cleaner
  Loctite Corp.

Dirt Devil
  Royal Appliance Mfg. Co.®

Endust®
  Sara Lee Household

Future Floor Finish®
  S.C. Johnson & Son, Inc.

Goo Gone®
  Magic American Corp.

Great Glass Cleaner
  CCP Industries®

Grout Brush
  Rubbermaid®

Holloway House Lemon Oil®
  Holloway House, Inc.

The Home Depot®

Iron Out®
  Iron Out, Inc.

Kitchen Brush
  Suburbanite®

Kitchen Scraper
  Norpro®

Lime-A-Way®
  Dist. by Reckitt Benckiser, Inc.

Lysol® Antibacterial Hand Gel
  S. C. Johnson & Son, Inc.

Lysol® Disinfectant
  S. C. Johnson & Son, Inc.

Magical Mop
  PVA Magical Mop™

Moen® Faucet
  Moen, Inc.

Mop & Glo®
  Dist. by Reckitt Benckiser, Inc.

Murphy Oil Soap®
  Murphy's Oil Soap™

Old English® Scratch Cover
  Dist. by Reckitt Benckiser, Inc.

Orange Clean®
  Orange Glow International

Magical Mop
  PVA Magical Mop™

Pledge® Furniture Polish
  S. C. Johnson & Son, Inc

Pure Power Amonia
  Dist. by Tops® Markets, LLC

Putty Knife
  Shur-Line®

Riccar® Vacuum
  Riccar America

Safety Glass Scraper / Mainstays Projects™
  Allway Tools, Inc.

Scotch Brite® Scour Pad
  3M® USA

Scrubbing Bubbles® Bathroom Cleaner
  S.C. Johnson & Son, Inc.

Soft Scrub®
  The Clorox Co.

Spic And Span®
  Procter & Gamble

Stanley® Duster
  Stanley Products

Starfiber Mop®
  Ecostar

Swiffer Mop
  Proctor & Gamble®

Swivel Scrub
  Tech Clean Products®

Vegetable Brush
  Rubblemaid®

Wal-Mart® Stores, Inc.

Weekly Planner
  Payne Publishers, Inc.

Webster®
  Sunshine

Weiman W Cook Top®
  The Herbert Stanley Co.

Windex®
  S. C. Johnson & Son, Inc.

Zud Heavy Duty Cleanser®
  Dist. by Reckitt Benckiser Inc.

Some of the pictures in this publication are from
Hemera Photo Objects®, Big Box Art®, and Corel Professional Photos®

Table of Contents

Table of Contents

Dedication:

In loving memory of my dear mother
Ruth Ellen Reese
1915 - 2002

Introduction

Why the demand for housecleaners?

The world we live in today demands much of our time and money. The rising cost of living has pushed many women into having to work outside the home just to make ends meet. Even two-parent families often have both adults working to keep up with the lifestyle they've become accustomed to.

Working women find it very difficult to cope with the demands of their job, as well as the responsibilities they have at home. Just preparing the evening meal and doing the supper dishes can seem like a tall mountain. Add to this the laundry, ironing, shopping, and a host of other duties, and you can see how things can overcome them.

Others have run their households quite well for years, but are suddenly thrown into a different situation, needing help to ease their burden. Some homemakers for one reason or another just can't cope with cleaning their homes.

Many elderly suffer health problems that prevent them from doing things they used to, such as caring for their home. Then there are those who just do not like cleaning at all. These are often the type of clients that hire a housecleaner and keep them employed for many years.

Houseclean for others

There are many persons, men or women, who could develop the skills to hire out for some type of cleaning. Often a husband and wife will work as a team cleaning houses or commercial facilities. Sometimes women haven't acquired any special training in a secular career because of raising a family and caring for their own home. Being divorced, widowed, or other changing circumstances often force women into the work field. Often young people just out of high school are confronted with a slow job market. Becoming a housecleaner might be something to consider as a job choice.

The fact that many women have to work brings on a great demand for housecleaners. Do you want to try out cleaning for someone? It's the kind of job you don't have to stay permanently committed to if you find that you are not suited for it.

This kind of work has many advantages! Adjustments in hours can be made to work around other obligations in your life, such as, dropping your children off at school. Housecleaning can be done in the morning and your other duties and errands in the afternoon. You may find that just a couple of cleaning jobs each week are enough to supplement your income.

This book is designed to give helpful ideas on how to get a housecleaning job, how to price it, and cleaning tips to do a professional job to keep the client happy. Or, you can learn additional tips to improve the cleaning skills you already have.

As you gain more experience your skills will improve. Don't let all the following information overwhelm you. After you clean for a period of time, it will become natural for you to do things a certain way. You'll learn a routine that will help keep your work consistent. Learning product usefulness and cleaning methods will reduce time spent while maintaining the quality of your cleaning. Suggestions are made, but to what extent you clean and how many extras you do when cleaning for others, you will have to decide for yourself.

Men and women alike, after a hard day's work, enjoy walking into a sparkling clean home with lingering smells of polish and cleaners. What a great feeling! As a cleaner you may also experience satisfaction. Step back, look at your work, and see how nice the house looks before you close that door.

Clean your own home

Many people like to clean their own home and just need a little help to do it an an orderly, efficient manner. There are others who want to hire a professional. Perhaps your housecleaner could pick up additional points to make certain tasks easier and improve their skill level in cleaning your home.

Do you need a little help to improve your housecleaning skill? Learning the usefulness of cleaning products along with some cleaning know-how could free up valuable time for your other pursuits and duties. Do you hate housecleaning? Why?

Often women cannot clean the whole house in one day. Is the lack of cooperation by family members the problem? Have them pick up after themselves so that you can spend your time cleaning instead of removing dirty clothes, drinking glasses, and dishes from their bedrooms. This teaches children responsibility to care for their personal space. This house preparation would be a necessary routine before the arrival of a housecleaner. Perhaps you need to do laundry and change the beds on a day other than the day you clean house. Maybe it's the preparation beforehand that wears you down. Think out what the real problem is. Is it the lack of help, good planning, time, or energy?

I truly hope the following information can help you simplify your life and aid you to have a 'squeaky clean' home!

Carol J. Klima

Chapter 1

How to Get Jobs

Ways to Get the Job:

- Run an ad in your local newspaper
- Tell existing jobs & friends you're looking for more jobs
- Referrals from other cleaning clients
- Distribute flyers
- Post business card on store information boards
- Other house cleaners pass on jobs
- Put an ad in any small free local paper or brochure

What works in one area, may not work in another part of town. Once you are established as a cleaner and have a reputation of being a *good trustworthy* housecleaner, from time to time you may get referrals through your happy customers. Often they brag to their friends about their great housecleaner.

Running a newspaper ad is usually the quickest way to get jobs. This way you are not relying on others and waiting too long a time to increase the income you need now.

Newspaper Advertising

Run an ad under: **Situation** (Position) **Wanted Domestic**

Check your newspapers for these type ads and look for wording that you think may appeal to prospects in your area.

Advantages of a small local weekly paper:

- Only get calls from certain areas you want to clean in
- Not so far from your own home
- It may charge lower fees than a major city paper

Call classified. Have your credit card ready to pay if phoning in the ad, or stop at the newspaper's office to pay. They request prepayment on ads for people looking for work to guarantee payment.

Have your wording written down and ready to give when you call. They often offer suggestions of wording if you need help.

Mention the particular city areas that you prefer to clean in, if you can stay within the word limit. Include your area code with the phone number. The client likes to know that the cleaner does not live too far away and will show up at the time expected.

Put the top heading **"Housecleaning"** in bold letters. It's an eye catcher and will add about a dollar to your cost. The householder will probably read all the ads first anyway, then start calling the most desirable or the one who lives the closest.

Call your ad in early that week and do not wait until the last day and hour deadline. First callers are usually listed first. When the paper lists the headings in alphabetical order, then you may wish to use a heading like "Cleaning-houses" or "A-1 Housecleaning," in order to be at the top of the list.

When to advertise:
- Before spring cleaning time
- Fall or a couple months before holidays, although jobs can be gotten any time of the year
- Advertising on a holiday week may not be as productive

Many newspapers allow 15 words for a set rate and charge more per word or word groupings over that number:
- Stay under the paper's limit to keep the ad fee down
- You will give clients more detail when they call
- Some papers require the ad to run in two local papers, each with several areas. This can make the price vary.

If you don't get calls from the newspaper ad:
- Wait a couple weeks and try again
- Did you choose the right paper?
- Rewrite your ad to make it more appealing
- List time of day for calling
- Too much competition:
  If there are another 10 -12 ads, your calls may be few, if any! When there are only 3-6 ads, the people will probably call all listed. Some will clip out the ad, hang it on their refrigerator, and call in a week or two after thinking about it or discussing it with their mate.

Check out the sample ads on the following page and incorporate the best words to fit your situation into one ad.

Sample Ads for the Newspaper

Housecleaning
Want good housecleaning? Affordable rates, experienced, free
estimates, western suburbs. Pamela (phone number)

Want Mrs. Clean?
Housecleaning at its best! Affordable rates, experienced, free
estimates, western suburbs. Judy (phone number)

Quality housecleaning
Good, trustworthy, weekly cleaning, reasonable, 4 years experience,
references, Valley, Eastland area (phone number)

Cleaning - Houses
Professional housecleaning, experienced, free estimates, bonded,
reliable, insured, South suburbs, call Melissa (phone number)

A-1 Housecleaning
Cleaning by expertise, trustworthy, references,
free estimate, call weekdays after 2:00 pm. (phone number)

Expert Cleaning
Husband, wife team, no house too large, trustworthy,
references, flexible hours, bonded (phone number)

Clean Team
Honest, hard working couple clean with expertise!
We clean homes or businesses, (phone number)

General Housecleaning
I'll clean your home with loving care! Honest, hardworking,
reasonable, call Sandy (phone number)

Post Ad or Business Card

Store information boards:

Put up a small ad or a business card with your phone number. Be creative. Use bright marker colors to get their attention or a colored file card with black marker to print. Keep it brief because they walk past quickly! Check the samples below. Be sure to take your own pins, tacks, or clear tape to hang the card.

Housecleaning
Weekly or bi-monthly, reasonable rates, honest,
Call Becky for a free estimate
(phone number)

Spring-Cleaning by a Team
One time shot - no job too big!
Free estimate, quality cleaning
(phone number)

Good housecleaning!
Need help? I'm the best!
10 years experience
(phone number)

A-1 Housecleaning
Quality cleaning at its best!
Area resident - call Rachel
(phone number)

Professional Cleaner
Dependable, experienced, reasonable rates,
Friday available! Call Cara at (phone number)

Flyers

Flyers can sometimes get you a job:

- If you have a computer, you can make up an attractive flyer.
- Check for pictures in clip art to jazz it up.
- Use a catchy phrase or slogan.
- Keep it professional looking.
- Give the impression that you take your work seriously.
- Keep it simple and to the point to grab the householder's interest quickly. They are not going to want to read a very wordy sales pitch.

Xerox the flyer:

- Xerox a 101 copies at a local office supply store to get a lower rate, about 4 cents.
- Their employees usually run these off for you.
- Form a flyer on the top half of a page and duplicate in on the bottom. This gives you twice as many flyers. They will cut them in half for a small fee.

Distribute flyers:

- Don't put flyers in mailboxes or mail slots in doors, as that is illegal, and you could be subject to a fine.
- Don't walk across lawns when distributing your flyers. This could discourage them from calling.
- Put the flyer inside the storm door quietly, or secure the flyer with a rubber band to the door handle. This will keep it from blowing away in the wind and littering the neighborhood.
- Have some dependable young friends help in distribution.

Sometimes flyers do get a response, but newspaper ads are more effective and less hassle. This will vary depending on the area you're planning on cleaning. You may want to clean in an area other than your own community, due to more jobs being available elsewhere.

Sample Flyer

Housecleaning
by a Professional

- 15 years Experience
- Reliable & Honest
- Reasonable Rates
- References
- Free Estimates
- Own Transportation
- Weekly or Bi-monthly

(000) 555-0000

Call Pat

Business Cards

On your interview, hand the person a business card if you have any made up. It's not necessary, but it makes you look very professional.

Design a business card:

Design your own card on a computer, even if it looks plain and ordinary, it will serve the purpose.

Buy the proper sheets of blank cards at an office supply store to create your own business cards. One box contains 25 sheets, 10 cards per sheet totaling 250 cards. Make up only 2 to 4 sheets at a time, then if your phone number changes, you won't be stuck with multiples of cards with the wrong information on them.

Use a picture on the card to immediately convey your type of business. A mop, vacuum, bucket, or a person scrubbing a floor may be in a clip art program you own.

Choose a catchy business name or slogan to make them remember you.

If you don't have a computer, perhaps a friend would help you design a card.

Many printers are available that print up cards inexpensively. They will be glad to help you with wording, pictures and layout.
You may be able to save money by comparing prices.

Professional Housecleaning

Let me make your home squeaky clean!

Weekly or bi-monthly

Call Carol

Reasonable rates
Experienced

Free estimates
(123) 555-0000

Phone Interview

Conversation with the client:
- Have a friendly voice.
- Carry the bulk of the phone conversation.
- Your voice tone and enthusiasm can prompt a more positive response from them.
- You want them to know you really like your job. This gives them confidence that you are a hard worker.
- Always thank them for calling, even if it doesn't work out with this caller.

Make a list of pertinent questions and comments that you can refer to and leave by the phone for when the calls come in from the ad. I suggest the following list. Laminate the list to have for future calls. Keep it near the phone.

Phone Interview

Where do you live?
Weekly or bi-monthly?
Size of house?
How many bathrooms?
How many bedrooms?
Family room?
Square footage?
Pets?
Children?
You supply cleaning products (client)
What kind of vacuum?
I do weekly cleaning, not spring cleaning, although I do extras.
Hard worker, I do good work!
Free estimate on interview
Set interview appointment time
Reference phone numbers (If asked for)

Appointment:

They will want to set a time to meet you. Have days and times in mind that you might suggest an appointment. Be prepared to be flexible. The sooner you can get on the appointment the better, before they schedule someone else in first.

Sell yourself:

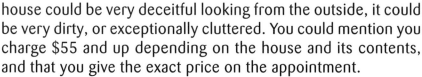

Let them know you work hard. People want to hear that their bathrooms will be sparkling clean, with streak-free mirrors. Mention that you do detail work, cleaning around knobs, corners, and cracks of things.

Payment:

Never give an exact price over the phone for a house you have never seen inside. The size of the house could be very deceitful looking from the outside, it could be very dirty, or exceptionally cluttered. You could mention you charge $55 and up depending on the house and its contents, and that you give the exact price on the appointment.

Those who want to pay by the hour usually pay small wages. Let them know you charge by the job, not by the hour, because you don't waste time. There is no reason to spend more time doing the same amount of work when you can do it in a shorter period of time. Most people just want a job well done.

References:

Most people do not ask for references, but you should have two or three names and phone numbers ready, in case they are needed. The householder may have an accountant who will insist their client asks for references.

If you don't have any past experience, give them references of people who know you as hardworking and trustworthy.

House Interview

For many, the hardest part of getting the job is the interview. You may feel intimadated or shy about talking with the people, but once you conquer that first interview, you'll most likely find they are very nice people. Many who call you will be just average hard-working people that just can't cope with housework along with their secular jobs.

Clothing:

Dress casual, modest, clean and neat. Blue jeans are okay because they expect to see you in this type of clothing.

Be punctual:

Be on time for your interview! Inform the client that you are punctual for cleaning time. The client appreciates your showing up on time when they are waiting to let you in the house before they leave for work.

Be friendly:

Tell them some of the things you do as you look through the house. Tell them a little about your family too. This will help them get to know you and trust you in their home. Don't mention this is your first housecleaning job, unless they ask.

Observant walk-through:

Have them show you the house first. Take a good look around for added things that might make the job more complicated. Notice dirty shower stalls, faucet build up, hard water problems, dirty baseboards, cobwebs, full-length mirrors, loads of knick-knacks, waxed floors to strip, walls full of pictures, animal hair on furniture, greasy range tops, lots of glass and patio doors.

Job assessment:

There can be jobs that appear hard, but just need a learned routine to simplify them. You may learn to like the job, and find it wasn't as bad as you first thought. Some people don't expect you to clean certain areas of the house they don't use often, such as spare bedrooms, or an unorganized office that is stacked with paperwork.

Expensive figurines and glassware:

If they have a shelf or area that has expensive pieces, you may want them to care for it themselves. They usually will agree.

Check the shower:

Don't be afraid to say, "May I check the shower to see what cleaning products it will require?" Open the curtain or shower stall door. Notice mold or soap build up around the faucets or tile, calcified water around sink faucets, or dirty door tracks. It may take you one or two hours, or even longer, at the initial  cleaning to get the main bathroom in good shape. Return cleaning will be much easier after that.

If they have two and a half bathrooms, but the master bathroom has a tub and separate shower stall, you have to consider it as three full bathrooms. Some large tubs with water jets are more difficult to clean, yet others are very easily wiped. Sometimes spare bathroom tubs aren't used. Wipe with Windex.

Make them aware:

Let them know you open certain closets and vacuum into them, especially walk-in closets. If they have certain areas they don't want you to clean, they will inform you. They may even have a room full of stored items they won't want you to clean.

Notice flooring:

Does the kitchen floor need wax stripped off? That can be very hard and time consuming. If it's really bad, you may need to spend the whole first time just getting the kitchen in shape. If they have linoleum floors, ask if they are 'no-wax' and what products they've been using on them. Does the bathroom have ceramic tile with dirty grout that needs scrubbing? Many newer homes now have easy to clean floors. They will let you know if you have to use a special cleaner.

Learn from the householder:

You can pick up helpful cleaning ideas from your client. They may have tried many cleaning products on something in particular and have learned what works best. Make a note of this. Some houses will have unique things you may not be familiar with. They may be able to tell you how to clean them.

Basic housecleaning:

You are there to do their basic housecleaning, not straighten up after them, or do their spring-cleaning. Tactfully mention they will need to put their personal things away, and straighten up the house before you arrive. Dishes should be done and the beds should be made. Tell them if they do this, you will be able to do a better job of the heavier cleaning.

Most people will have their little areas of things they need handy for usage. They will usually tell you not to bother moving these piles of items or stacks of papers. You might even suggest they put them into small basket or plastic containers that can be moved easily.

Cluttered house:

Ask yourself, will this house stay fairly clean until I return, or will it be totally trashed when I come back in two weeks? If they have children who are not trained to put rubbish in wastepaper baskets, and objects and clothes are strewn all over the floor, this may be the usual condition of the home. You may not find out until you've cleaned a couple times. If they won't straighten the house before you come to clean, you may not want the job.

Be alert to ideas:

Ask if it's okay to use polish on their furniture. Make a mental note of things the householder mentions that might be a hang-up. They may tell you they had a cleaner before who wouldn't knock down cobwebs, shake rugs, clean hand prints off the patio doors, move items when they dusted, or clean smudges around light switches. Remember these little things that bug them, and make sure you always clean these things in particular. This will help you keep the job.

Spare rooms:

They may have you clean the spare bedrooms only before they have guests coming to stay.

When in the kitchen mention things you clean:
- Shine all the countertops and appliances
- Remove faucet buildup
- Top of refrigerator
- Range top, suggest they wipe up daily spills
- Inside microwave
- Wipe down cabinets
- Mop the floor

Don't do items:

Inform them you don't normally do inside range ovens, fireplaces, or refrigerators. You also don't want to wash dishes, do ironing, laundry, or change bed sheets.

Curio cabinets or large hutches are often in the dining rooms. These often contain many delicate or costly items behind glass doors. Let them know you do not clean the inside of these. Some will empty the hutch out and have you clean the glass doors and shelves. They put the contents back in themselves later. They may want to do this once a year.

Laundry:

If you agree to wash a load of towels or sheets charge an extra $5.00. Try to avoid this, or make it worth your while.

Changing beds:

Don't change beds unless they want to pay you extra. Changing two or three beds is hard and time consuming. If you agree to this, you could ask for $10-15 extra.

Sit & talk:

After you've looked around the house on the interview, sit down and talk with them briefly. They will want to get to know a little about you, like where you live, are you married, and do you have children. It will make them feel more comfortable about you. This also gives you a little time to think about how long it will take you to clean in order to quote a reasonable price.

If they have agreed to hire you, check their supply of brushes and ask if they have a caddy. Offer to buy the caddy and brushes for them. By doing this you can purchase the exact items you will need. They may cost from $10-12. They will give you the money and are usually glad you'll do this for them. Check the "Equipment List" (see page 21) at the client's house for needed items.

Be regular and reliable:

Let them know you are reliable, that they can count on you. Do not cancel any more than necessary. They often plan parties and events around the time the house is cleaned. Mention you would appreciate their regularity, as you rely on this income.

When they go on vacation, they might even have you clean while they're gone. You might offer to clean out their kitchen cabinets. This way you don't lose your regular income during their absence. You would need to discuss a way to get into the house if you don't have a key or garage code.

You don't particularly like the job:

Options:

- Let the people know you want to think about it. You may even change your mind if you don't receive other calls.
- If the house is too large, tell them it's too much for you to handle.
- Suggest they hire a couple that work as a team.
- You may want to give it to someone you know.
- Price it very high, they either won't hire you or you'll wind up with a good paying job that's worth the effort.
- If you take on a job you don't like, you can always replace it with a better one later. If you are desparate for work, you might want to put up with the job temporarily. Maybe you'll learn to like it. Use it as a learning experience, and then pass it onto someone in need of a job, unless it's *very bad*. Just inform the client you can't handle it any longer. Always be kind when releasing them so a bad word doesn't follow you.

Checklists

Take the following list with you on the interview. Check your "Reminder List" before you leave the client's house so as not to forget something important. They will be impressed that you are so organized. Have them show you where they store their products, brooms, step stool, rags, vacuum belts, bags, and the vacuum cleaner. This list will help remind you.

Reminder List

Straighten up house
Discuss product list
Polish okay?
Don't do: inside refrigerator, range oven, fireplace, dishes, make beds, laundry or ironing.
Discuss product supply list
Bucket
Mop
Broom & dustpan
Money for caddy & brushes (if agreed)
Rags, wash with bleach, no fabric softener
and not too much laundry detergent
Set price
Paid in cash
Extra first time ($20)
Work phone numbers (For emergencies)
Where are vacuum, bags, & spare belts kept?
Trash bags,
Where are products stored?
Step stool?
Set exact time & starting date
How to get into house?
Appreciate regularity!
Park in driveway, which side?

Discuss cleaning products:

Check your list of products with the client's supply. Have them purchase products before your first cleaning. Having the right products can make your work easier. Request easy-to-use spray containers. Carry your own spare cleaning products in the trunk of your car, in case they forgot to buy something. Especially your first time in a house, you don't want to waste time fighting with inadequate products. All these products may not be needed on every job. Also other brand name products may be preferred.

Product Supply List

Windex
Antibacterial kitchen cleaner
Comet
Bon Ami
Soft Scrub
Clorox Clean-Up
Scrubbing Bubbles
Toilet bowl cleaner (liquid)
Zud (for hard water)
Lime-A-Way
Clear ammonia (*NOT* cloudy, or lemon)
Liquid Spic And Span
Murphy's Oil Soap
Endust or Lemon Pledge Polish
Goo Gone
Toilet tank tablet
Future Floor Finish
Mop & Glo
Wax stripper
Brillo Pads
Scotch Rite Scour Pads

Homemade solutions:

Some make their own cleaning solutions. This can be time consuming. In our busy world most prefer to buy ready-made products to make cleaning simplified. Have the client buy clear ammonia, which can be used to clean many things, as there is no soap in it. Other detergents can be added to it, if and when needed. Be sure to read the section on safety tips, don't forget to **READ LABELS BEFORE MIXING PRODUCTS, ESPECIALLY THOSE CONTAINING BLEACH, AMMONIA, OR ACID.**

Equipment List (At client's house)

Vacuum
Stepstool
Bucket
Rag or sponge mop
Long-handled Swivel Scrub
Lots of rags
(Cotton, linen, or washcloths, towels, diapers)
Soft-edged broom
Dustpan
Caddy
Toilet bowl brush for each bathroom
Floor scrub brush (Stiff bristles)
Two vegetable brushes
Narrow grout brush
Long-handled duster
Dust mop
Swiffer Mop
Starfiber Mop

Determine which mops will be necessary for each client.

Equipment Information

Brooms or dry mops:

Soft-ended bristle brooms are very good at vacuuming up fine dust and crumbs. The Swiffer Mop is especially good for smaller rooms and is easy to store because of the size. There is also a larger sized Swiffer mop. These can be purchased at Wal-Mart. Dry cloth dust mops may be dampened to use on hardwood floors.

The Starfiber Mop is great for larger floor areas because the width of the base cleans a lot of area quickly. It can be used dry or dampened, will flatten to clean under low pieces of furniture, and is very easy to use and maneuver. The pad is washable.

MADE BY: ECOSTAR®
(888) 333-1158
WWW.CLEANHEALTHY.COM

Wet mops:

Rag mops allow you to get closer to the baseboards and underneath kitchen cabinets easier than with a sponge mop. A new rag mop may need to be soaked a few minutes before using, to make it more absorbent.

SOLD AT TRADE SHOWS
WWW.TYCITY.COM

The Sponge Squeezer, PVA Magical Mop absorbs large amounts of water quickly, use after scrubbing with the Swivel Scrub shown on the next page. It's great for quick mopping.

Buckets:

Many plastic buckets are made with an additional insert to remove excess water from a rag mop. If the mop leaves excessive water on the floor, then you may need to use a sponge mop instead. Some buckets are rectangular shaped and are necessary when using a 12 inch sponge mop.

To dry a floor faster, throw a towel rag on the floor, scoot it around with a mop, long-handled brush, or your feet.

Brushes:

A scrub brush with firm plastic bristles will clean more thoroughly than one with softer bristles that tend to bend sideways and loose its proper shape.

When shopping at various stores, watch for anything in the line of brushes, scratch pads, and cleaning equipment that might help you in shower stalls or other problem areas.

The Swivel Scrub is a long-handled scrub brush that can help you avoid getting on your knees. It's very maneuverable around furniture legs, appliances, and the toilet. Someone who can't get down on their hands and knees to clean will find this especially convenient.

SOLD AT WAL-MART®
MADE BY
TECH CLEAN
PRODUCTS®

Vegetable brushes:

Vegetable brushes are great for cleaning in the bathroom and kitchen, around faucets, drains, knobs, window frames, and metal straps. Have two, use the white one in the bathroom and a colored one in the kitchen. Have this same system at each job and you won't get the brushes mixed up. This is more sanitary and lessens the spread of germs to other areas of the house. Use brushes with bristles similiar to the brush shown on page 24.

Tile & grout brush:

Pictured below is a narrow brush with stiff plastic bristles. Its size makes it easier to clean tight areas around faucets, toilet seat knobs, or window and door tracks.

SOLD AT WAL-MART®
MADE BY RUBBERMAID®

KICHEN BRUSH
BY SUBURBANITE®

Rags:

Rags are better to use than paper towels. Folded rags can be refolded to prolong usage. Inform your client how to wash the rags with the following directions:

- Use Clorox bleach along with a lesser amount of laundry detergent. Too much detergent will not rinse out and cause streaking on mirrors.
- The rinse cycle should be with cold water.
- Don't use any type of fabric softener or laundry sheets. Softeners inhibit absorbency and can cause streaking on glass and mirrors.

Pre-folded cloth diapers without foam, washcloths, 100% cotton t-shirts, and hand towels make great rags. Baby receiving blankets or flannel make terrific dust rags.

Scheduling:

If they ask for every third week, this will disrupt your schedule. Often you can talk them into every other week (bi-monthly). Explain this as the usual routine for most housecleaners. A once-a-month job may also ruin your schedule. This is the request from some elderly people, as their houses do not get very dirty, or they can't afford to pay twice a month. If you get a job in an apartment, have them tell others you're available.

House entry and exit:

Discuss how to get into the house and how to lock up. Often people require or need a certain day of the week when it is more convenient to let you into the house, or a time before they leave for work. Others may trust you with a key or code to enter through the garage door. Some will leave their door unlocked for you, or leave a key somewhere outside.They may ask you to leave certain lights on when you leave after cleaning. Make a quick note so you don't forget these requests.

Choice of day:

Some entertain on weekends and want the house clean for company. Others actually prefer Monday or Tuesday, after all the company has gone home, so the house will stay cleaner a longer period of time.

Leave a note:

Check their supplies before leaving each time cleaning. Let them know you will leave a note when products need replacing. They will appreciate not having to do this themselves.

Pricing the Job

Pricing the job is not always easy, as all houses and the contents vary. If you are not sure, price it $5-$10 higher than you think. You just might get the job anyway. If you start out too low, it's awkward to have to raise the price right away. If they don't want to go that high, you could drop a little or they may have you not clean certain spare rooms they don't use. Set in your mind a minimum you'll take for the job.

There is good money to be made at cleaning, but the clients want their moneys' worth. Most people don't mind your spending a shorter period of time as long as the job is done well. Don't promise a certain amount of time, although you may be able to approximate how long it will take you. Some days it may take you longer if you're not feeling up to your normal spry self. Set yourself a slower pace that day.

Houses are usually dirtier than they seem. Take your time in looking through the house thoroughly. Even then, you will be surprised at the areas that are dirtier than you imagined. Many times a house that appears spotless, will still be time consuming cleaning, because you have to clean all areas again, even though they appear clean.

You will most likely spend more time cleaning the first time than you planned. Check the shower stall in the bathroom, as it is usually the culprit that will monoplize a lot of your time. Leave them a note that you will catch anything missed the next time.

Charge by the job:

If someone wants to pay you by the hour, they usually don't want to pay you very much. One who cleans many hours and works by hourly rate isn't necessarily doing a better job, but possibly just spending more time to make more money. Charge a flat rate for the job and do not charge by the hour. This is standard procedure for housecleaners as well as commercial jobs.

If you are a fast worker and can do quality work, then you can be making anywhere between $15-$25 an hour. A lot will depend on how good you are and if you are able to keep up a steady pace. Fast isn't good if you can't do the quality. If you're just starting at housecleaning, it may take you a little time to catch on as to how to cut your time and still do a good job. As you improve your skill, your time will gradually lessen.

Sample pricing:

For a three-bedroom ranch, two full bathrooms and family room, with 1,800-2,000 square feet, you might charge $60. Without the family room, charge $55. Some cleaners won't work for less than $50 even for a small house. These are not unusual rates. A two-bedroom, one bathroom small apartment may merit $40-$45. A small one bedroom apartment, you may get about $35-$40 depending on its contents. If you are fast with your hands you may be able to clean a three-bedroom, two-bath ranch house in two and a half hours. If you work fast, don't neglect routine things. Find a pace that is comfortable for you and yet allows you to do good quality work.

Charging extra:

The first time you clean a house you should charge extra, generally $20. The reason for this is that you will be cleaning more thoroughly and spending more time than a regular cleaning visit, and the house will most likely be dirtier than you had anticipated. It may take 2 or 3 visits cleaning to get the house in proper shape. People don't mind the extra fee but expect a good job. Another reason is that if they use you for a one time cleaning and then quit, which is rare, at least you got paid a fair price for your work. If you do inside and outside windows that are easy to clean, such as double paned windows of a ranch, you may charge them an extra $15. For a lot of windows $20 would not be out of the question. They would pay a window cleaner a lot more than that. The client would probably hire a professional window cleaner for a very large house. They often clean their screens too.

Large House:

Some large houses may merit a fee as high as $75-$125. An extremely large house will require even higher fees. Very large houses are hard to price. You have to put the price so high to make it pay, that you may be better off cleaning two small houses for the same amount of time and make more money. The house pictured below would likely be in the price range mentioned above.

Teamwork:

You might try working as a team with another housecleaner, someone who keeps a similar pace as yourself. If you partner with someone that doesn't work as well or as quick as yourself, you may be doing the bulk of the work. In that case, you would be better off working alone, or paying the other cleaner a flat rate that is less than half the fee. You might want to team up with someone just for a very large house and still work alone cleaning smaller homes. Often a husband and wife will work as a team cleaning very large homes.

HUSBAND
& WIFE
WORK
TOGETHER
AS A TEAM

Commercial cleaning:

If you eventually expand to cleaning commercial buildings, medical offices, motels, restaurants, banks, or other businesses, they often require night workers, as well as weekend nights. You may make more money, but would have to change your sleep habits and perhaps sacrifice your weekend entertainment time. Apartment buildings require cleaning during the daytime after a certain time like 8:00 or 9:00 AM so as not to wake-up tenants too early. Even though this book concentrates on professional housecleaning, many of the cleaning tips can be used in commercial cleaning too.

Price Quote:

Give them an exact price on the interview. If they like you, they will usually hire you on the spot. If they wait to call you later, often you never hear from them. Don't pass up another good job for someone who doesn't get back to you right away.

Indecisive householder:

If they can't seem to make up their mind to hire you, try to figure out why. Is it the price? Maybe they think you live too far away. Reassure them that this is no problem for you. Maybe they don't like the day you have open! Perhaps you can put them on a temporary day, with the intentions of moving them onto a better day when the next opening comes along.

Payment:

Request they pay you in cash. It's easier than trying to run to the bank often. If you decide to take on several jobs a week, you will appreciate the cash even more. Getting paid on the day you work is especially nice for day-to-day expenses.

Established Jobs

Price Increase:

If you have cleaned for the same people for many years, wages have changed. Over a period of years you should gradually raise your fees. As they make additions, buying more furniture, adding more glass, you will find it harder to clean. This would be a good time to raise the price. How do I go about doing this? What should I say?

Mention, "if you don't mind, I need to raise your price by $10. I usually make $60 for this size house now." Maybe even settle for just the $5 raise if they're hesitant.

A job you were paid $35 ten to fifteen years ago, is most likely a $55-$60 job now. If you're still cleaning for that low rate, try to make a substantial raise. If the client doesn't raise your wage, run an ad in the newspaper to pick up a new job at the current rate, and then replace the old one.

Trade off:

Sometimes you can do a trade-off or bypass part of the house, if the client wants a particular thing to be cleaned that you don't ordinarily do. Perhaps they want the inside of the refrigerator cleaned that day because they're having guests over. Try to work out some kind of compromise that both of you will be happy with. Maybe they will pay you extra that day.

Complainers:

Once in a while, you may work for someone who looks for something to complain about each time you are there. Perhaps the whole house is beautifully cleaned. Some people are never happy no matter how much you do, they want more from you. There are too many nice people to worry about one complaining client. That kind usually quit eventually anyway.

If you have several clients complaining, truthfully analyze the quality of your work, and try to improve where your skills are lacking. Learn from your mistakes and avoid repeating them.

If they let you know that you missed something last time, say you're sorry, and try to remember that item each time you are there to clean.

Unprepared house:

You may come across someone who will regularly not prepare the house. These jobs are not worth the hassle and they rarely change the habit. Replace it with a better job or charge them more for the extra work. Occasionally, a regular job may have to rush out and not prepare as usual. This is different! You try to help them out. They may even leave you extra money that day for your added effort.

Can you cope with a client who continually leaves messes as pictured below? Straightening the house is different than the housecleaning itself. Everyone in the family should cooperate, preparing their own room before the cleaner arrives.

Helpful supplies:

A skilled worker needs the proper equipment and products to do the job right. Prepare a bag so you can carry the following list of necessary supplies into the job. Others can remain in the trunk of your car.

Supplies to Take on the Job
Goo Gone
Plastic putty knife
Butter knife
Small scissors
Long-handled nylon duster (or yarn type)
Hand sanitizer (in car)
Window razor
Rubber or vinyl gloves (extras, too)
Water resistant bandages
Vacuum
Vacuum belts
Vacuum bags (in car)
10-15 ft. extension cord
Screwdriver
Spare rags in trunk
Kneeling pads
Contact cement
Appliance touch-up (white)
Notebook & pen
Small squirt bottle window cleaner
Couple window rags (in bag)
Plastic bag for dirty rags
Sweatband

Many of these supplies won't be needed all the time, but when you do need them, you will be glad you planned ahead. You might want to carry your own vacuum in the trunk of your car for a back-up in case the client's vacuum stops working.

How Can These Supplies Help Me?

Goo Gone:

Use on many items to remove glue, sticky labels on glass, plastic, and scuffmarks off linoleum. For labels, remove the paper of the label first with a hot wet rag, or by rinsing, and then apply Goo Gone. Let it set on the sticky part for a couple minutes, allowing the solution time to work, then rub off with a rag or paper towel. (Sold at Wal Mart and Home Depot, made by Magic American Corp., Cleveland, OH)

Plastic putty knife:

A plastic putty knife is safer than a butter knife as it will not scratch. This can be used for cleaning between counter top edges next to the range where crumbs accumulate. There are also plastic kitchen scrapers that can be used for various things.

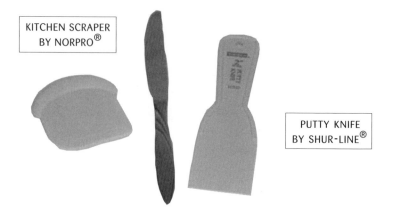

KITCHEN SCRAPER BY NORPRO®

PUTTY KNIFE BY SHUR-LINE®

Butter knife:

Use an old butter knife to clean the edges of the metal strips that divide rooms with carpet from linoleum to get out old wax and dirt buildup.

Wrap a rag around a knife to clean out tight areas in window, patio, or shower stall tracks. Beware: a metal knife will scratch a procelain sink, chrome, or toilet bowl.

Small scissors:

Toilet tank tablets are sealed securely in a wrapper. Use the scissors to open them. You might need to trim a long thread coming up from carpeting so the vacuum doesn't catch it and pull out a row of stitching. Cut up a large old bath towel to make more rags. Washed rags sometimes tangle up together and need cutting apart.

Long-handled nylon duster:

This type of duster is quite handy and reaches high areas. It can be sprayed with a little Endust to make it more effective. Check to make sure it's removing the dust properly; there may be some items that it won't dust efficiently, but leave streaks. The nylon type duster can be washed and will last a long time if you don't get it against a light bulb.

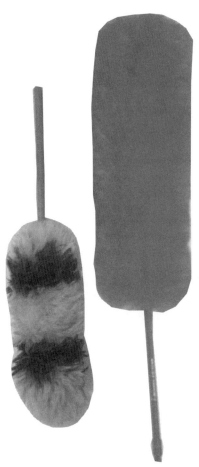

Other dusters:

Lambswool dusters are nice, but are more costly. A medium length yarn or nylon duster can stick out of your back pocket and be handy to grab, if you forgot to dust something earlier. Feather dusters may be used, but pick up any feathers that fall.

Hand sanitizer:

After cleaning bathrooms and before you leave the job, be sure to wash your hands with soap and water. Carry hand sanitizer in your car for the times you may forget to wash before leaving.

Window razor:

Use a Safety Glass Razor that retracts back into the handle. Remove paint spots or other ugly spots from mirrors or windows. When using anything that is sharp, be careful not to cut yourself! Sold at Wal-Mart in the paint section.

Bandages:

Use bandages for those small cuts you'll get on your fingers to avoid leaving blood spots and to protect yourself from germs. Purchase a brand that resists loosening when getting wet. Wear gloves when working with water.

Rubber or vinyl gloves:

Gloves are a necessity to protect your hands from chemicals and bacteria. Wear rubber gloves when cleaning toilets, areas in the bathroom, and the kitchen sink. There are different types of vinyl gloves. Choose a glove that will allow your hand to be flexible and comfortable.

SOLD AT WAL-MART® GARDEN OR PAINT DEPT.

Chemical gloves are heavier and last much longer. You really get your money's worth from them.

Heavier gloves may be washed and hanged to dry. If you get moisture inside the gloves during usage, after a time they can get musty smelling.

Medium weight vinyl gloves may be sufficient. If you buy inexpensive gloves, they may tear easily and will not last as long as a better quality pair.

Thin, disposable gloves tend to make the hands perspire, but will protect you from germs. Those who clean medical offices use disposable gloves because they can throw them away after one use and grab a new germ-free pair.

Vacuum cleaner:

You may prefer using your own vacuum. Power driven vacuums are easier on the back to use, but heavier to carry. Use their vacuum, if possible.

If your client's vacuum works well, it can save you money and wear and tear on yours.

Which vacuum should I buy?

Your client may ask you this question. Recommend a good quality vacuum, such as the Riccar model 8850, as pictured. It's an excellent upright vacuum with good pickup and on-board tools that have powerful suction. It's easy to use, has a long cord, and ultrafiltration bags that captures allergens, germs, spores, pollens, dust mites and bacteria. It has dual fans and internal metal parts that reduces constant repairs and replacement. Riccar also sells a vacuum for commercial use.

Vacuum bags & belts:

When using your own vacuum, always have a supply of bags and belts in the trunk of your car. If you're using the client's vacuum, make sure you know where they store these items. Don't get caught without a working vacuum, because it gives the house that final touch.

Extension cord:

Some newer vacuums are now made with very long cords, so an extension cord might not be necessary. Even some of the nicest large homes are lacking a plug outlet in the main hallway upstairs, forcing you to replug into every bedroom. A ten to fifteen foot extension cord may be sufficient.

Screwdrivers:

Use a screwdriver to pop up a drain cover on the shower floor or bathtub to clean out dirt and hair, tighten toilet seat bolts, clean dirt out of a corner, or old wax along floor metal strips. One regular screwdriver and one phillips head would be sufficient for most situations you might encounter.

Pliers:

A bottle will sometimes have a lid so tight, that it can't be removed by hand, such as, appliance touch-up paint.

Rags:

Never be without rags! Cleaning a whole house with paper towels will take you longer and be costly. Have the client supply the rags, if possible. This will eliminate extra laundry for you, and added usage of your appliances and detergent. If you wash their rags in your washer, always use bleach to kill germs.

Always have extra rags in your car trunk in case the client forgot to wash their supply. If they are on vacation, you might want to use your own rags. They won't want to return to smelly rags sitting in a bucket .

Kneeling pads:

Kneeling on ceramic tile and other hard floors can be painful to the knees. After a period of time the knees will start to hurt and give you regular problems if you don't take care of them. You may want to buy kneeling pads that attach with velcro. Check for these at discount or home improvement stores in the hardware section or among work clothing. You can also buy a large single kneeling pad or make one. These are more inconvenient as you have to keep moving it as you're scrubbing.

If you're handy with a sewing machine, try making your own kneeling pads that slide up the leg and stay on your knees during the whole job. You will find they are more comfortable than the store-bought kneeling pads. Computer mouse pad material is thin, but very dense, giving more protection to the knees than thick foams.

Directions to make:
- Cut computer mouse pad into two 4 x 5 inch rectangles.
- 24 inches of black 3 inch wide elastic, a thinner leg will not need as much.
- 2 pieces heavy muslin or blue jean material 8 x 9 inches. Wrap the material around the mouse pads, leaving extra material on the sides where the elastic will attach.
- Remove the pads. Turn material inside out and stitch the bottom edge, angling the side ends of the material to the size of the elastic. Turn the material back to the right side.
- Insert mouse pad, turn under the raw edges.
- Attach the elastic to one side of the material, wrap around your leg and pin the other side to comfort. Make it snug, but not so tight to cut off your circulation. Stitch the elastic to the material.
- Use a sewing machine needle for heavy material to avoid breaking the needle.
- The kneeling pads can be hand-washed, flat dried, or you can toss them in the dryer.
- Even if your sewing job looks crude, remember the whole idea is to protect those knees!

Contact cement or glue:
Glue can be used if you break something. Be sure to tell the client of the breakage, how it happened, and that you glued it. If they are not home, leave them a note and apologize for anything that is your fault. They will appreciate your truthfulness. Use clear all-purpose glue or contact cement. You want something that dries quick and holds tight. There are many brands to choose from. Keep the glue in a plastic bag in case it seeps out.

Small bottle window cleaner and a couple rags:

This is handy when you're leaving and have forgotten to clean the storm door. This eliminates two trips back to the utility room.

Appliance touch-up paint:

This comes in a small bottle with a brush applicator and is usually white. Use it to cover white chipped porcelain on a sink, range, or washer, dryer to cover the ugly black spots. Other colors are also available. This can really make a difference in appearance. Many people are unaware of this touch-up paint.

Notebook and pen:

Leave a note for products they need to buy. Say thanks and draw a little smile face to brighten their day! Don't get in the habit of writing notes all the time. Just leave a note when supplies are getting low. You don't want them to get into the habit of always leaving you a note asking for a lot of extra things to be done. An occasional thank-you note from them is nice.

The above items are not all necessities, but are handy to have when you need them. You will also need the following items.

Small address book:

Record your client's address, phone numbers, pagers, and their work numbers for emergencies. Have these with you.

Have cash:

Sometimes people don't have the correct amount of money to leave you. It's best to always have a five and ten dollar bill with you for change, if possible.

Weekly planner calendar:

Have a weekly planner calendar to keep track of your jobs, especially if you plan on cleaning several homes. Hang this up on a wall that makes it easy to check daily. Fill in your calendar three or four weeks ahead of time. If your client calls to change their day, it's convenient to have that already filled in. Plan ahead for holiday changes.

Prepare to clean:

You will ruin your clothes at times from bleach products and your pant knees will wear quicker than usual. Also wear clothing that you can maneuver around in easily, and something that won't get caught on knobs. It is advisable to wear a cooler top if you are prone to getting hot while you're working.

If you perspire heavily, you may want to consider wearing a sweatband so as to avoid dripping wet spots on their furniture.

Tennis shoes or a good pair of walking shoes is advisable for comfort. It's safer to wear shoes while working, especially while vacuuming, as long as the client doesn't object.

At the job:
- Prepare the caddy with all the needed cleaning products and brushes
- Get a trash bag to empty wastebaskets
- Place your duster and rubber gloves in the caddy
- Put the clean rags in a bucket to carry with you
- Have the vacuum out
- Put on your kneeling pads and you're ready to work!

Steps to Start a New Job

Get the job:
- Run an ad in a newspaper, post cards, distribute flyers, inform friends you're looking for jobs
- Have phone interview notes by the telephone
- Note available dates you could clean

Phone interview:
- Discuss phone interview list
- Set an interview appointment as soon as possible

Prepare for interview:
- Dress casual, modest, clean, and neat
- Take with you: paper, pencil, weekly calendar, business card, and your reminder, product, and equipment lists

On the interview:
- Be on time for the interview
- Introduce yourself and hand them a business card
- View the house first
- Set the price
- Set the date to start cleaning
- Check your lists: reminder, product, and equipment

Home preparation:
- Buy any supplies you're purchasing for them
- Put in trunk; vacuum, belts and bags, cleaning supplies, supply bag, cobweb chaser, rags, and a spare mop
- Plan ahead a routine to clean

On the job:
- Ask any questions before the client leaves the house
- Have a set time limit for your first visit, clean thoroughly
- Check supplies, leave a note for products needed
- Take your wages
- Lock up the house as instructed

After the job:
- Record earnings, gas mileage, and any expenses incurred

Chapter 2

Cleaning Room by Room

Kitchen

Dust first:

Dust first on the things you can use a long-handled nylon duster, such as: chef rack, top of refrigerator, blinds, pictures, clocks, wine rack, ceiling fan and higher up items. By dusting first, you will not cause dust to settle on newly cleaned surfaces.

READ PRODUCT LABELS AND
CHAPTER 6 ON SAFETY TIPS

Countertops:

Never slide the caddy on a countertop. Anything rough on the bottom of the caddy could scratch the countertop.

It's important to use antibacterial cleaners to kill germs. Smooth and bright colored counters are easily wiped with an antibacterial product or even Windex. Always use a clean rag. Don't use their dirty dishcloth because it contains a lot of bacteria. Put their dish rag in the cabinet under the sink.

Clorox Clean-Up can remove stubborn stains from many things. Dirt can accumulate in the seams at the back of the counter and backsplash, around metal straps, or the raised edges around the sink. Scrub these areas with a brush. Use Clorox Clean-Up on a counter that is white or almond colored. It can also clean white grout between tiles. Spray on the grout, let the solution set 1or 2 minutes, and then scrub, rinse and dry.

If you leave a rag with bleach laying on the counter, it may leave a permanent bleached spot. When working with a bleach product, always put the bleach rag in a bucket, caddy, or in the sink. Don't set a wet bleach bottle on a colored sink.

Some countertops may have leather-look indentations that collect dirt in the cracks of the pattern. In the past, these were often installed in white and almond colors. Spray with Clorox Clean-Up and use a stiff bristled scrub brush to clean the grooves. Test a small inconspicuous spot first when trying a new method of cleaning you're not familiar with. The same type of countertops in colors can be scrubbed with Spic And Span mixed with a little ammonia. Be sure to rinse and dry to shine.

The owner may request you to use a specific kind of cleaner on their countertops or polish, which also need to be shined or buffed. This can be time consuming and not something to be done often. Antibacterial sprays will help to shine counters, as well as killing many germs.

Don't use powdered or liquid cleansers on counter tops. They can cause dull spots that will show when the light reflects.

Items on countertops:

Use Windex or antibacterial sprays to wipe down items that are on the counter tops, such as cutting boards, can openers, canisters, coffee makers, trivets, glass bottles, mixers, fruit bowls, blenders, teakettles, paper towel holders, toasters, spoon

holders, knife holders, salt and pepper shakers. Move these items and clean under them, because there will be crumbs and spills. Wipe any cutting boards on the top and bottom, and the counter underneath.

Can openers:

Occasionally clean the can opener more thoroughly by spraying with Clorox Clean-Up at the cutting blade area and brushing to clean. Don't cut yourself on the blade.

Toaster:

Unplug the toaster before wiping down to avoid electrical shock. Empty the crumbs out from the bottom. If the toaster doesn't open on the bottom, turn it over above a wastebasket. Most toasters can be cleaned with just glass cleaner. A stainless steel toaster can be cleaned with liquid cleanser to remove grease. Wipe the direction of the grain on the metal to avoid scratching. On the side of the toaster you will be wiping back and forth sideways, not up and down. If you try to use a mild dry cleanser, test out a spot on the back first to make sure it doesn't cause fine scratching. Use a damp cloth.

Use Goo Gone to remove any burnt-on melted plastic from bread wrappers. Apply the Goo Gone, let it set a couple minutes and rub off. Don't let the solution run down inside the toaster. Repeat the procedure for a more stubborn spot.

Telephones:

Wipe off telephone receivers and untangle the cords. Elderly clients appreciate this. Often makeup and hairspray accumulate on the receiver. Wipe it with a damp cloth and a disinfectant

type cleaner, Windex, or Clorox Clean-Up. Don't use an overly wet cloth to avoid electrical shock and damage to the phone or answering machine.

Coffeepot:

Unplug the coffeepot before cleaning, unless it has a clock and timer set. Throw their used coffee grounds in the garbage, not down the garbage disposal. Rinse and dry the glass pot with a clean dishtowel. Wipe the coffeemaker base down with Windex or Clorox Clean-Up to remove dark stains.

Glass coffeepots can be cleaned with Lime-A-Way or Comet to remove stains or calcified water. Wash the pot with soap afterward and rinse well. The bottom of the pot may be cleaned by this method too, but do *not* use cleanser to scrub the outside where the numbers and lines appear, as these might scrub off.

Sponge and dishcloth:

Sponges harbor a high bacteria count. Some people wet the sponge and microwave it for about thirty seconds or a little longer, to kill the germs. Dishcloths also harbor bacteria and should be laundered with Clorox bleach. Change to a clean cloth daily and anytime you wipe up uncooked meat juices.

Light switch plates:

Use Clorox Clean-Up or antibacterial cleaners to clean the light switch plates. Windex or ammonia would also leave them streak free. Do not let any liquid get into the electrical part of the switch to avoid shock or a short.

Wallpaper:

Some light wallpaper can be wiped with Clorox Clean-Up to get off stubborn spaghetti sauce stains and other spots. Rinse well. Ammonia mixed with a little Spic And Span is good for cutting grease splatters caused from range top cooking.

Tables:

Tables may need to be polished if they are wood. Laminated tables can usually be wiped off with a window cleaner. Be sure to wipe the side edges. Protect wooden edges with polish.

Glass tabletops can be cleaned with straight clear ammonia, Windex, or Great Glass Cleaner. Be sure to check underneath, especially near the edges where children leave fingerprints. Look across the glass, toward the light reflection, to locate any smears or streaks, and re-clean if necessary.

White laminated tables often stain and can be cleaned with Clorox Clean-Up. For stubborn stains let the solution work for a couple minutes and then wipe off the solution.

Clean metal tables with a damp cloth and no soap, and wipe dry. If you can use mild dish soap, they will let you know.

Chairs:

If they have wooden chairs in the kitchen, ask what they like them to be cleaned with. Heavily polished chairs can get unsightly old layers of wax and dirt. Endust maybe a good choice to cure this problem. There are many wood cleaning products made for your finer woods, with two step cleaning and polishing.

Vinyl covered seats can be wiped with Windex. Whatever you use on the chairs, don't leave anything on them that would ruin their clothing when they sit down. Many chair seats, legs, and rungs can be dusted off with the long nylon duster. Never set eyeglasses on a chair, someone might sit on them.

Cabinets:

Some kitchen cabinets need furniture polish. Painted or laminated surfaces need only to be wiped down with Windex to be streak-free. Use something that won't leave a soap film.

Always wipe around the handle areas. Clean the top edges of the doors when needed. Open the cabinet doors under the sink area, wipe around the edges where handprints and dirt collect. If the wastepaper basket is kept under the sink, you need to clean all around that area, as many throw garbage in the basket and miss the target.

Some older kitchen cabinets are difficult to clean, perhaps the homeowner can inform you of what works best.

If you need to use furniture polish, you may not want to do them from top to bottom each time you clean, this is hard and time consuming. Wipe the problem areas regularly, and wipe them down totally every three or four months, or as needed.

Clean the kitchen cabinets just before mopping the floor as you may cause dripping down the doors when cleaning the sink. Wipe away cobwebs under the bottom edges of the cabinets.

Wipe the areas of cabinets under an island, drawers, doors, and where bar stools are used by young children.

Remove trash:

Empty wastebaskets into a trash bag as you move from room to room, or you can go around and empty all of them before you start to clean. Empty all the ashtrays, wash them and put them back in the same area you took them from.

Check for wastebaskets under the kitchen sink and bathroom vanities, many people like to store them out of sight. Wipe the kitchen wall behind the wastebasket or cabinet floor to eliminate splatters.

Keep their recycling containers separate from the garbage, if this is their habit. A plastic kitchen wastebasket can be cleaned with Clorox Clean-Up; it kills odors, germs, and removes ugly stains. Spray the lid, let it set for a minute, and then scrub with a brush. Rinse, dry, and insert a new plastic liner.

Don't get into the habit of taking their garbage out to the curb for garbage pickup, unless it's necessary for someone who is unable to do it themselves. This is not part of housecleaning. If the client is in a wheelchair or has bad arthritic hands, this would be a nice gesture to help them out. Put the trash bag into their garbage can. When the house has an attached garage, the garbage cans may likely be stored there.

Gas range:

Soak range top grates and trays in hot water with automatic dishwasher soap. Let these soak for a few minutes while you are cleaning other things in the kitchen, allowing time for the hot water and the strong soap to soften up stubborn burned on areas. After soaking, use a steel wool or Scotch Brite pad to clean. Stuck-on grease spots should clean off easier from the grates.

Under the trays of older type ranges, use a grease removing product. Spray it on and let it set a couple minutes to help dissolve the grease. Ammonia with soap could also be used. Wipe out lowered grease catching areas and use a steel wool pad or Scotch Rite Scour Pad for heavy duty scrubbing on the stubborn spots that are not on the top porcelain.

Always use regular Soft Scrub on the porcelain part of a range top. Shake the bottle before using. After cleaning, shine with window cleaner to remove any streaks. Don't use harsh cleansers as it would harm the surface, leaving permanent dull spots.

With a newer range you want to be more careful with the surface. Many have the sealed burners and the range will be very easy to clean. The burner cap may be soaked in hot water and cleaned with Soft Scrub or a steel wool pad. For stubborn spots around the burners, use this short tightly bristled brush along with the Soft Scrub. Wipe with window cleaner to remove any streaks. Check the kitchen utensil section at Wal-Mart.

SOLD AT WAL-MART®
MADE BY
RUBBERMAID®

On a gas range, the knobs can be pulled off and scrubbed with a brush and Soft Scrub to remove stains. Again, don't use steel wool pads on the porcelain or glass part of a range. It would scratch the surface.

Older ranges may have metal straps on the top sides; clean these areas with a cleaner and the grout brush, or use the plastic putty knife. Little detail work neatens the appearance.

Clean the top edges of both the oven door and the bottom drawer with Windex, as these areas often attain drip spots.

To clean underneath a range without pulling it out from the wall, remove the bottom drawer. First take out the drawer contents, then remove the drawer, pulling it out and tipping upward to pick it up out of the roller track. Set it aside and then clean the floor. Put the drawer back in with the handle end upward manuevering the rollers back into the track, lower the drawer down level, and roll it back in. This is not necessary to do on a job. The client will like this helpful suggestion.

Dirt often accumulates around the sides of the range next to the counter. Use the plastic putty knife, scraper, or wrap a rag around a butter knife and run it through the slot. If the area is too tight, lean your hip against the range pressing to make it move a little so you can run the wrapped knife through quickly.

Be careful not to spill water down the front of a newer gas range. Near the top edge of the oven door there is often an open vented area that runs clear across the top. Anything dumped down into the area runs between the layers of the door and can only be cleaned by taking the door apart with a screwdriver. The client will need to clean this area.

Electric range:

Ranges with a smooth glass cooking surface have special creme cleaners for the top surface as the one pictured here. A small amount of the solution works well.

Don't use powdered cleansers on the glass cooking surface. The client will probably tell you what product was recommended by the manufacturer. Never try to clean a hot surface. The client may wish to care for the range top themselves.

The control areas on many ranges get very stubborn greasy spots. Use clear ammonia on a rag or brush to clean around the knobs on the glass, but don't get too much moisture on the digital pad, it could cause problems. Make sure you haven't turned any burners on by mistake.

When cleaning the range, don't forget to wipe the ovenhood, not only the top surface, but also up underneath where food and grease often splatters. Ovenhoods can get a nasty grease build up over a period of time if it doesn't have regular cleaning. Don't use a steel wool pad, it would scratch. Use ammonia with soap or Clorox Clean-Up to clean the metal surface.

Refrigerator:

Abrasive cleansers are not meant to clean the surface of a range, dishwasher, or a refrigerator; they will leave a dull spot. Wipe these areas down with window cleaner to shine.

Clean the top of the refrigerator with soap water and ammonia or Windex to remove any grime. In between, regular dusting may be sufficient at some homes.

Clean the handles on the sides that show, and those on the backside where the hand grips around. You don't ordinarily clean inside the refrigerator, but you can open the lower door and wipe the top edge of the door and the bottom base edge inside on a standard refrigerator as just a quick touch-up. This is not necessary on a side-by-side model.

Condenser coils:

A condenser coil cleaning brush reaches under the refrigerator farther than the vacuum can reach with the crevice tool. The grill has to be removed first. Brush, then vacuum. Suggest to

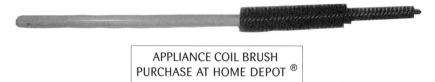

APPLIANCE COIL BRUSH
PURCHASE AT HOME DEPOT ®

the client to buy this or vacuum around these coils a couple times a year to prolong the life of their refrigerator. Some people never clean the coils, but the compressor needs this air flow. Service fees and a new compressor can be quite costly.

Water dispensers:

Refrigerators that have ice and water dispensers have a water reservoir area to catch dumped water. These areas get calcified water collection that can be stubborn to clean. Remove the water from the reservoir with a rag. Apply Lime-A-Way, let set a few seconds, and then scrub with the kitchen brush. Wipe away the cleaner and shine with Windex. Take the little plastic grate over to the sink, spray with Lime-A-Way, clean with a brush, rinse off with water, dry, and replace.

When ice cubes have a distinct unnatural taste, the problem might be solved by the following method. Turn off the icemaker. Remove the ice bucket from the freezer. Throw out the bad tasting ice. Spray the ice bucket with bleach or Clorox Clean-Up and let set a couple minutes. Wash, rinse well, dry and return it to the freezer. Turn the icemaker back on. This may take care of that problem. If you don't desire to do this for a client, you could inform them of this cleaning method. Is there a filter that needs to be cleaned or changed? The client takes care of this.

Some new side-by-side refrigerators have a small door section that holds a bottle of milk and a couple other things; it saves on electricty when you avoid opening the large door numerous times. Open and wipe the inside of this door and around the chrome edges before shutting because these areas get dirty.

Dishwasher:

Windex the front and clean around the control knobs with ammonia and the kitchen brush. Wipe the top edge of the lower front panel. This area is often very narrow. Try using an ammonia rag wrapped around a butter knife or putty knife to fit through this tight area. Clean with Windex, the top and side edges where the dishwasher seals, because these edges show on the outside of the appliance.

Open the door of the dishwasher to wipe around the top and side edges on the inside occasionally. These areas collect a lot of splatters when items are turned upside down when loading the dishes. This area doesn't usually get cleaned when the dishwasher runs because of the way the door shuts and seals.

Microwave:

Notice where the "clear" or "stop" button is located on the menu pad before cleaning the microwave. In the event it turns on while you're wiping the control pad, you will be able to quickly turn it off to avoid damaging the microwave.

If the microwave inside is constantly splattered, suggest they buy an appropriate cover made for reheating foods. For quick reheats, many people often use a paper towel or an inexpensive paper plate which covers, but doesn't stick to the food. Note that these should not be used for long term cooking to avoid catching on fire.

Wipe the inside of the microwave with a warm dish soap cloth, Windex rag, or something mild. Be careful not to cut your fingers on the small plastic rack holders on the side walls. If you use sprays, don't let the fluids run down into seams. Some brand microwave ovens have a cardboard cover inside at the top, don't soak this with too much water.

Glass turntables can be removed and washed with warm soap water. Stubborn stuck foods like cheese will need to be soaked in hot water a couple minutes, and then use the plastic scraper. When there is food stuck on the walls, you can microwave a cup of water for two minutes to make these wipe off easier. Use the plastic scraper or putty knife if needed. If you use a knife or razor, you risk scratching the surface. Burnt popcorn can leave a nasty smell. Remove odors by heating lemon juice.

Clean an over-the-range microwave before you clean the range because you may be dropping crumbs down on the range surface, making extra work. A small grease filter is underneath the microwave that should be cleaned monthly by the client. Use hot dish soap water, not ammonia, as it might discolor the metal.

A very porous white plastic surface on the outside door area that has stubborn yellow spots, may be removed with Clorox Clean-Up and the white stiff bristled brush that is shown on the bottom of page 49. Rinse off the solution. Clean both sides of the handle with an antibacterial cleaner. Clean the outside door control pad with a damp cloth, and nothing harsh that would scratch or take off the printing. If the microwave is a small countertop model, slide it over and clean underneath to remove dust and crumbs. Don't try to move older heavy models that are on limited counter space.

Sink:

Clean the sink just before mopping the floor, as you will be using it to clean other things.

Most clients will tell you not to use harsh cleaners on a new stainless steel sink. Use Soft Scrub, or a mild nonabrasive cleanser like Bon Ami, unless your client instructs you not to use *any* type cleanser. Some may request Scrubbing Bubbles. Shake the can before using. Many porcelain and stainless steel sinks can be cleaned with Soft Scrub, Bon Ami, or Comet Cleanser. Just antibacterial dishsoap can be used daily for in between cleaning to kill germs and to quick shine. When using Soft Scrub, shake the bottle first to keep the solution mixed. Don't get water by the holes on top of the cleanser cans.

Porcelain sinks can often be cleaned with Soft Scrub, Comet, or Bon Ami for regular cleaning. Zud Cleanser is good for sinks with hard water problems, rust stains, and will clean off fine scratches that some of the other products can't.

While cleaning the sink, clean the soap dispenser squirter with a brush, and also the dishwashing soap bottle cap if they leave the bottle on the sink. You might want to put the bottle, dishcloth, and other things like this under the sink to neaten the appearance.

USE VEGETABLE BRUSH
AROUND FAUCETS

Lime, calcium and rust cleaners:

Spray Lime-A-Way around the base of the faucet fixture and by the edges where the handle rises. Seconds later brush away the dirt with ease. Rinse well with plenty of water so no acidic solution is left on the chrome. Please read the labels.

Use the vegetable or narrow grout brush around the sink edges, metal straps, and drain. Remove the metal drain strainer; clean the inside and the bottom. Brush down into the drain and into the rim seams, as these areas get dark stains.

Rubber mats used to protect the sink can get ugly stains. Wet the mat, sprinkle with Comet cleanser, and spray with Clorox Clean-Up. Let this set a couple minutes to let the bleaches work, scrub with a brush, and then rinse both sides with water. This even brightens up the colored mats. If there is stubborn stuck-on food, soak it with hot water to soften, then brush.

After cleaning any type sink, spray with Windex, wipe dry, and shine the chrome.

White appliance touch-up paint can be used to hide badly chipped black porcelain spots in sinks or other appliances that are white. Paint a thin layer, let it dry, and apply another thin coat, if needed. Too much paint might set in a glob. Keep a paper towel handy when applying, in case you don't like that first application, wipe it off quickly. Other colored appliance touch-up paints are available in the hardware section of stores.

Garbage disposal:

If there is garbage in the disposal, run water, and turn on the disposal until it's eliminated. Remove the black rubber drain liner, brushing clean, the top and bottom with antibacterial or disinfectant soap. Or you may spray this with Clorox Clean-Up, but rinse with plenty of water so no bleach remains on the rubber. Some types of garbage disposals have permanently fixed rubber parts that can't be removed. Reach in with a vegetable brush to clean the bottom side of the insert. Clean the brush with bleach.

Garbage disposals get odors, especially in the summer months. Squirt a germ killer down into the interior of the disposal to help remove odors, but rinse off rubber parts with water. Some grind lemon and orange peels to lessen the smell.

Never stick your hand down by the disposal blades. If the switch isn't flipped totally off, it may suddenly come on. This has been known to happen. Use tongs to pull out any rag or object that has dropped in by accident.

Ceiling fan:

Ceiling fans need regular cleaning when they are used a lot, especially in the summer months. The side of the fan blade cutting into the air seems to attract most of the dirt. Use a Spic And Span rag with a little ammonia to wipe down occasionally. When cleaning the blades with a rag, use your other hand to steady the blade. Don't apply much pressure on the blade and cause it to break off.

In the winter months, regularly use a long magnetic duster to dust the blades and light fixture. You can often bend the end six inches of the duster into a form that is easier to move across the blades. Bend the duster back into its proper shape when finished.

Throw rugs:

If a rubber backed throw rug is stuck to the linoleum due to moisture or wax, soak it briefly with warm water to loosen, and slowly pull up the rug. To prevent this from happening, lay rugs down after the cleaned floor has dried, or wipe the floor dry with a towel rag as you clean to speed up the drying process.

Shake rugs outside to prevent more dust from floating through the air. Shake both ends to remove the maximum amount of dirt. A very old or delicate rug may not hold up to a vigorous shaking. Some firm and flat rugs can be vacuumed, but be careful not to get the ends caught up into the rotating brush.

Refer to the section on flooring for more information about cleaning the various types of floors throughout the house.

Bathroom

Doing a great job cleaning the bathroom will help you to keep the job! Men and women alike, love to see a sparkling, clean bathroom. The smell of cleaners lingering in the air gives them the secure feeling of a germ-free environment.

Equipment:

Use your caddy to carry your cleaners and brushes to and from the bathrooms and the kitchen. Set the caddy on the floor. Have your bucket full of clean rags so you won't have to stop and go for more.

Exhaust fan:

Check the exhaust fan and see if it is clogged with dust. Turn it off to clean, and use a long-handled brush, broom or cobweb chaser to knock down the dust before starting to clean the rest of the bathroom. You could also use an extension vacuum attachment with the small dust brush end to reach up by the ceiling. This would eliminate clumps of dust falling down on everything.

The plastic grills on the exhaust fan are easy to take down to clean, but they usually have two sets of wires that have to be squeezed to insert back up into the fixture. I suggest not taking it down at someone else's house, because you might spend more time trying to get it back up properly. It can be tricky!

Turn the exhaust fan on while cleaning the bathroom to keep yourself cool. Air movement also helps the mirrors dry quicker when cleaning.

Bathtubs:

For a bathtub that will clean easily, use Scrubbing Bubbles or another soap scum remover. The aerosol can is quick to use and easy to spray evenly across a surface. Shake the can often. Spray the dirtier areas first to allow more time for the cleaner to work. Spray with Windex, wiping to a shine. Don't mix bleach and ammonia products. Rinse any excess foam down the drain. Rinse all cleaning products down the drain to avoid fumes forming in the event the client adds a drain cleaner afterward.

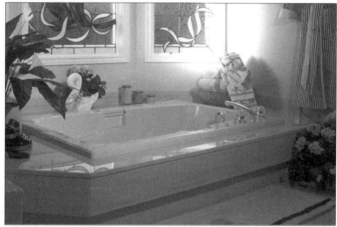

Stand on a rag when inside or outside the tub to maintain sure footing. Some tubs may be easy to reach to clean without having to step into them. Just a little moisture on the floor can cause your feet to slip because of your leaning inward.

Neglected bathtubs may need to soak with cleaners a few minutes. Someone cleaning motel bathtubs should also try the following method to whiten tub bottoms. Wet the tub first. Sprinkle with Comet cleanser and spray Clorox Clean-Up around to whiten. Let set a few minutes, then scrub. This method can help porcelain or fiberglass showers. Very stubborn stains may take three or four times soaking to restore the white color. Zud cleanser may also work well. Bad mold stained caulking at edges of tubs may need to be removed and recaulked. Spray Clorox Clean-Up on any sign of mold developing. Shine the outside of the tub last, as it usually gets splattered while you're cleaning.

Use Zud cleanser on bathtubs that have very stubborn water stains caused by hard or iron water. Wet the tub, sprinkle Zud around, and let it set before scrubbing. Bleach products may cause an orange or yellowing color to appear when applied and then you have to use the Zud to get that off, creating more work.

If a product is removing the finish on the tub, use a less abrasive product for the regular cleaning. A refinished bathtub has a delicate surface and may need something very mild to be used on it, like a soap scum removing product. The client was likely infomed what to use when it was refinished.

If you need to remove old decals from a porcelain bathtub, you might try putting very hot water in the tub to soak first to soften the adhesive. If you use a window razor to remove the decals, be careful not to scratch the finish. For any glue residue left, try cleaning it off with Goo Gone or Clorox Clean-Up, letting the solution set a short time to work on it.

Shower curtain:

Suggest they wash the curtain liner in the washer on the gentle cycle and put in the clothes dryer for one or two minutes on warm heat, just to soften slightly. Hang it up immediately.

You can also spray plastic curtains with Scrubbing Bubbles and wipe down with Windex. Most of the soap film will come off. For stubborn mildew or moldy spots use Clorox Clean-Up. If you clean the liner while hanging, be careful not to tear it from the hanger holes. Hold the curtain against the shower sidewall to wipe down, or have a rag in each hand on both sides of the curtain. This would be considered an extra, something you don't have to do, but your client may appreciate not having to buy another liner right away. The client could take the liner down and place it flat on the floor to spray and wipe clean.

Knob dispensers and water jets in tubs collect dirt and soap that may need to be opened and cleaned with a brush. This is something the homeowner should notice when filling them. That would be a good time for them to clean these areas themselves, or you might check them every few months.

Shower stalls:

Showers stalls seem to be the hardest job to tackle. The first time cleaning will be the worst. The directions for bathtubs on page 59 can also be used in some showers stalls.

Throw a rag in the bottom of the shower to stand on, to keep your tennis shoes from slipping on the wet floor. Always keep at least one foot on the rag to maintain your balance.

If the shower stall walls are very dirty, apply Lime-A-Way and let it set to allow time for the solution to work. Be sure to wipe the cleaner around, or you may find random clean streaks where the product ran down. Let the cleaning product do some of the work for you. Clean the sink and the toilet first, and then scrub the shower. Try different products to see what works best on that particular shower. Use a nylon padded scrubber with a handle on the flat areas. These are good for using on fiberglass along with Lime-A-Way or Scrubbing Bubbles to remove soap scum. Use a brush for the seams, tracks, and other areas.

When you step out of the shower stall, remember you will have cleaning solution on the bottom of your shoes that will need to be wiped off before walking around. Lay a towel rag on the floor in front of the shower that you can step out onto when your done.

Clorox Clean-Up removes a lot of mold and often prevents the growth of more. Spray the grout, let it set, and then scrub with a stiff bristled brush. Sprinkle Comet Cleanser and spray Clorox Clean-Up on the shower stall floor, let set a minute and then scrub. Rinse well, and dry with a towel rag.

A squeegee left in the shower can be cleaned with Clorox Clean-Up and a brush to remove mildew or mold. After cleaning, wherever you see a tendency for mold growth, such as near the tracks or in the grout, give it a little spray. This will help deter more mold from growing.

On a regular basis you may be able to spray the shower stall with Scrubbing Bubbles (without bleach) and wipe down with Windex. If you use soap scum remover that contains bleach, then don't wipe down with a window cleaner containing ammonia. Read page 130 on product safety.

Stains on shower stall seats caused from shampoo bottle labels can often be removed with Clorox Clean-Up. Spray, let set, then wipe. For a stubborn stain, dampen Zud cleanser, let it set a couple minutes, and then firmly wipe with a rag.

Remove razors out of the way from the area you're cleaning.

Soap scum often accumulates on the soap holder and underneath. Use soap scum remover or Lime-A-Way and scrub with the nylon padded scrubber and brush the soapy grooves.

Spare bathroom shower stalls may not be used regularly. Wipe quickly with a Windex cloth to shine.

Glass sliding doors:

Windex the outside of the shower door before the inside. This makes it easier to see the dirt when cleaning the inside, and also aids in spotting anything missed on the outside.

Shower stalls with glass sliding doors that have towel racks or handles, one on the inside and one on the outside, can usually be reversed, one door passing by the other, to clean the narrow middle area of glass. If you can't get them to reverse, spray in that area a cleaner, then use the plastic putty knife wrapped with a rag, or flush the area with water.

Don't be removing the glass doors off the tracks if you don't have to. It could turn out to be very difficult to get them back in the tracks, and you wouldn't want to break one. In the event you knock one off the track by mistake, just raise slightly to get the wheels back into the track at the top first, then bring the bottom back in last and lower it into the track. Some doors are not this easily replaced in the tracks. It would be good for the owner to take the doors down yearly and clean the hidden areas and the bottom edges to get off any mold growth.

Comet or Zud cleanser on a wet cloth can be used in the shower door tracks. Rubbing back and forth will remove much of that black metal looking accumulation from the chrome. A degreasing product could possibly be used in the tracks as well, but rinse with plenty of water. Read the label before using so as not to damage anything. Use Scrubbing Bubbles to clean gold colored tracks. Harsh cleansers may remove or ruin the gold finish. If you use Lime A-Way, rinse the chrome off with plenty of water. Dry and shine the area with window cleaner.

When using soap scum removers in the shower or tub areas, the foam tends to get wiped towards the drain. Rinse down with water to prevent the foamy solution from collecting inside the drain.

Bathtubs and showers that are made as a four piece unit, have a seam at the top of the tub and bottom of the wall section that often accumulates mildew or mold growing underneath. Check under that edge, spray with Clorox Clean-Up, brush, and rinse. If you miss this area and it has black mold, they will see it when they lie back during a tub bath.

Occasionally spray Lime A-Way on the end nozzle of the shower sprayer, let set, and brush away the calcified build up.

After a Fiberglass shower stall or tub is initially cleaned, regularly use Scrubbing Bubbles, spraying it all around the shower, and then wiping down with Windex to shine. Don't use a window cleaner with ammonia at the same time if you're using a soap scum remover that contains bleach. *Don't* mix ammonia and bleach, it would form dangerous fumes. If you ever blend these two chemicals by mistake, hold your breath and step away. Get rid of the solution quickly, or if its on a rag, quickly rinse down the drain with water. To breath this in could be very dangerous. Refer to page 130 on product safety.

Slow drains:

If the water is going down the drain very slow, it's probably clogged with hair and dirt. Sometimes the drain cover can be popped up or unscrewed to clean out. If you do this, be sure to wear gloves, because this area will be heavy with bacteria. Spray Clorox Clean-Up in the drain to kill germs. Clean the drain out with a screwdriver. Use Clorox Clean-Up again, and brush the drain clean. Rinse with plenty of water. This will also take away bad drain odors. Wash your hands and gloves thoroughly a lengthy time with antibacterial soap. Clean the brush with bleach.

Hard water:

Very hard water can cause rust stains. Zud cleanser can help this problem. Apply liquid cleaners to a dry shower, let set, and then scrub in a few minutes. To use dry cleansers, wet the shower, sprinkle on the Zud, and let set for a short time. Scrub with a stiff bristled brush or a nylon scratch pad. Rinse well. These methods may need to be repeated for a shower stall that has been neglected for a long time.

Toilet:

Put on your rubber gloves before cleaning the toilet. Protect your hands from chemicals and bacteria. If you have cuts on your hands, it makes you especially vulnerable to infections. If you get rashes on your hands, you will want to wear gloves for cleaning even the sinks and shower areas. Certain chemicals or cleaners may irritate your skin if your hands are sensitive. Even healthy hands can get dry.

Before you clean the toilet, wipe the toilet paper holder, as it can be easily forgotten. If they have the holders that are inset into the cabinet, remove the toilet paper, clean the inside, and put the paper back in the holder, usually with the paper rolling from the top. If the paper is gone and you know where they keep their supply, put a new roll in for them. Check under their cabinet, main linen closet, or on shelves in the garage. If they have a basket or container used for holding spare rolls, refill this supply. They appreciate your saving them time.

Use a toilet bowl brush that has no metal parts to avoid scratching the porcelain. If the client has an old brush that the bristles are smashed on the bottom, and the metal wiring is exposed, have them throw it away. Buy the type pictured here.

First clean the inside of the toilet using a disinfectant cleaner, squirting the cleaner up under the rim all around the inside. Using a toilet bowl brush, brush up under the rim where the water flows in. If this area isn't thoroughly cleaned, it can hold odors in the bathroom. If the dirt in this area is very stubborn, try using Comet on a damp rag, wiping under the rim. Regular cleaning with a brush will keep this from returning.

If they don't have toilet bowl cleaner, you can substitute with Comet cleanser, a disinfectant, or one of the liquid floor cleaners. Some clients may request you to use Comet regularly in the toilet bowl. Shake excess water off the brush to store.

Flush the toilet after you have cleaned the outside of the toilet. This will give the chemicals plenty of time to kill more germs inside the bowl. Flushing after cleaning will keep a dirt line from forming at the top of the water's edge.

After cleaning the inside bowl area, clean the outside. There are many antibacterial or disinfectant spray products that can be used. Choose one that will not only kill germs, but leave a clear shine. If the cleaner leaves the toilet seat tacky, the client will not be happy. Rinse or wipe it with Windex. With a clean rag and disinfectant, wipe the flush handle, tank, and then the seating area. Keep refolding the rag to a clean part. Next clean around the seat hinges and the rest of the toilet base, spraying and brushing around the base knobs. This order of cleaning keeps dirt from being brought up onto the seating area. Double check the front base to make sure there are no run marks.

Clean the floor around the base of the toilet with a brush and cleaner. If there is no caulking, odors will remain if this area is neglected. Always use a clean rag to clean each toilet, to prevent spreading germs from one area to another. Don't use a dirty toilet cleaning rag to clean any other object. Lower the seat and lid for a nice neat appearance. Use a scrub brush to brush up the nap on a cloth toilet lid cover. It makes the bathroom look sharp.

Never use the water from inside the toilet bowl to clean the rest of the toilet or anything else.

Don't use bleach products on the top and front of the toilet tank. A cloth seat cover may get ruined when the seat is placed in the upright position. A bleached spot may appear later when moisture collects during a steamy shower.

Clean the toilet brush holder that sits out in the bathroom and empty any excess water to eliminate odors. If the brush smells, spray it with Clorox Clean-Up, let it set a couple minutes, and then rinse. If you can get them to keep a toilet bowl brush in its container by the toilet and the cleaner under the sink, it will free up more space in the caddy. They might not have room in the cabinet, or won't want chemicals where small children can get to them. Some parents install child safety devices on the cabinet doors.

When there is toilet paper in the toilet, flush it before cleaning, or the paper will get caught in the bristles of the brush.

If when flushing the water rises up to overflow, push the flush handle upward to stop more water from entering the bowl.

Some style toilets have a small hole at the bottom inside bowl, which may have a very bad dirt build up. You may be tempted to use a screwdriver or an old butter knife to loosen the dirt. *Beware!* The toilet surface can scratch. Some scratches don't clean off! You could turn the shut-off valve and flush the toilet to eliminate the water out of the bowl. This way you can clean the bowl with Zud Cleanser, Comet Cleanser, Iron Out or Lime-A-Way. Turn the water back on when finished. Read the directions on the label to use Iron Out for overnight soaking.

Toilet tank:

Clean the tank once a year. This will help to eliminate the black lines that form from the holes where the water enters into the bowl. Remove the toilet tank lid. Clean inside the tank with a liquid cleaner and a brush to remove any stains, mold, or sediments. Be careful not to break any flushing parts. Hold the flush handle down to remove all the dark water so it doesn't remain in the tank. Flush two or three times. Liquid Iron Out may be used for overnight soaking, but follow label directions.

Some people like to drop a cleaner tablet into the toilet tank to keep the toilet bowl cleaner on a regular basis. Many appreciate the cleaner smell, especially in the hotter summer months when odors tend to be stronger. If the homeowner goes away for the winter or a long vacation, and the toilet is rarely flushed, a bleach tablet should be removed to prolong internal rubber parts. They won't want to use a bleach tablet if they have a dog that sneaks into the bathroom to drink out of the toilet.

If a bleach tablet is used in the tank, do not use any product inside the toilet bowl with an acid or ammonia content. Use something compatible.

Sinks:

Clean the sink before doing the mirror so you don't splatter a clean mirror, then clean the countertop. Use Scrubbing Bubbles or mild liquid cleaners on gold fixtures.

DON'T USE
HARSH
CHEMICALS
ON
GOLD FIXTURES

Apply Lime-A-Way around a faucet fixture that has a calcified water build up. Seconds later brush away the dirt and rinse well with water so no product remains on the chrome. This process may be necessary each time you clean house for a client. This product can be used on various types of faucets.

Use Scrubbing Bubbles on bathroom sinks, as it is a disinfectant, leaves a nice odor, and is gentle to the hands. Spray it on, wipe it off with a rag or clean around the faucet and the bowl with a brush, then rinse down with water. Spray with Windex and use a rag to shine dry. Under the faucet handle, seesaw back and forth with a rag in any tight area where it's difficult to reach and brush underneath the faucet extension.

Wipe the wall by the sink to remove splatters. Try not to make any loose edges of wallpaper worse than it is.

Clogged drain:

To plunge a sink that is draining slowly, stop up the sink and put hot water in it to help soften whatever it is that is causing the problem. Place your elbow of one arm, holding a rag against the overflow drain hole, and the hand holding the stopper arm down so the drain stays open. This creates more pressure, forcing up some of the clogging material. Plunge with the other arm, keeping the hot water running. Don't burn yourself with water that is too hot. As you plunge, black mucky chunks will come up into the sink. Remove this with a glove and a paper towel. Be sure to disinfect the sink when done. Wash your hands and gloves thoroughly as this would have a high bacteria count.

This plunging, of course, is not something you have to do for a client, but you may choose to do so. Use this method at home in your own sink. Perhaps you can avoid the expense of a plumber.

Overflow water hole:

Clean the water overflow hole at the front of the bathroom sink. If the mirror is low to the sink, the reflection of this hole shows the dirt in the mirror, especially if the hole background is white. Use Lime-A-Way with a small bottle brush to clean, rinse well. Squirting some Clorox Clean-Up into the hole and cleaning it regularly, will also help to remove drain odors.

Countertops:

If there are open seams around the sink area, don't let excess water run down into them. It could leak inside the cabinet, ruin some things, warp the boarding, or mold could form.

The backsplash needs wiping, and a brush may be necessary to clean into sealed cracks where dirt collects. Also clean the small top edge of the backsplash. On almond or white counter tops, you may be able to spray Clorox Clean-Up and scrub with the kitchen brush, whitening these seams.

Some people hold the hairspray can far away from their head with the spray mostly falling on the sink and surrounding floor area. This is often stubborn to clean up and the floor can feel very tacky. Clorox Clean-Up cuts this stickiness. Test an area, making sure it's safe to use on the surface you're cleaning and rinse well. Goo Gone can also be used to remove sticky substances.

Clean items on the counter. Unplug the radio, blow dryer, or curling iron before working with the water to avoid electical shock. Any small mirrors that set on the counter, clean with Windex and scrub soap dishes. If a bar of soap is dirty, it can be brushed clean and rinsed off. Liquid soap dispensers collect globs of soap. Clean the dispenser area with a brush and rinse off.

Wipe any ceramic tile around the sink with Windex. Clean off perfume and aftershave bottles, lining up the bottles neatly by size. If they have accumulated too many bottles setting on the counter, put some of them down under the sink, leaving out the nice looking ones. Use Clorox Clean-Up in the bottom of a toothbrush holder to help kill germs and deter mold from forming. The enclosed type holder can be sprayed with Lime-A-Way. Let this set while cleaning the sink, and then use the small bottle brush to reach through the holes to the bottom. Rinse out with hot water running through it. The matching glass can also be cleaned with Clorox Clean-Up to kill germs.

Refold and straighten towels that are hanging sloppy. Wipe pictures with glass cleaner, as they can get splatters or run marks on them from a steamy room.

If you spray a soap scum remover on a glass item above the sink, be careful. It will be so slick it could slip from your hand, breaking the item or chipping the sink.

Cabinets:

Wipe the vanity cabinet or wall next to the toilet with an antibacterial spray. This will help eliminate odors. Lemon Pledge could be used on wooden cabinets to leave a pleasant scent and remove smudges. Windex is good for laminated cabinets and for quick wiping on some painted woods. Clorox Clean-Up works well for cleaning stains from laminated countertops and white cabinets.

Wipe the edges of cabinets, door handles, and baseboards with a wet rag to eliminate body powder messes.

Mirrors:

Turn the exhaust fan on while cleaning to help the mirror dry quicker. This also helps you to have a little air movement when working in a smaller room.

Always use a clean rag to wipe down the mirrors. A diaper is the best, or an absorbent towel rag. Spray on the Windex, Great Glass Cleaner, or other window cleaner, not letting it run into seams of frames or metal edges. Always clean the top half of the mirror first. While up high, dust off the light fixture. Don't lean on a sink counter top that is not affixed with a cabinet underneath, such as those above the toilet. If you stand on the toilet lid when wiping the mirror, keep in mind some seats are not attached tight and will slip out from under you very quickly. Don't step on a flimsy lid, it will crack or totally break.

Never stand on a porcelain sink. It could break and cause you serious injury and embarrassment.

Washing methods that cause mirror problems:
- Fabric softener used on rags can hinder their absorbency
- Softener dryer sheets might leave a residue on the rag
- Too much laundry detergent might not be rinsed out well
- Bleach was not used
- Rags were air hang dried and harsh

Mirror problems from other causes:
- Heavy cigarette smoke
- Hairspray
- Conditioner sprays
- Spraying wrong cleaning product on by mistake
- Wiping with a dirty towel or rag

To thoroughly clean a problem mirror, try using straight clear ammonia and wipe. Use your regular window cleaner after that. Check the mirror at another angle, particularly above the faucet area, as the way light reflects will show more missed areas. Check again in a few minutes to see if a film has developed.

Towel racks:

Towel rack arms that attach to the wall accumulate dust and grime. Wipe off with window cleaner on a rag. Don't use bleach products on these, as wet bright-colored towels may get ruined from bleach spots.

Light fixtures:

You may need to clean the light fixture in the bathroom. Check it each time you are there. Dust regularly and occasionally clean it off with an ammonia rag or window cleaner.

Some light fixtures need to have the bulb removed to clean the inside of the glass fixture. Always have the light fixture turned off. Be careful not to get shocked. Do not use an overly wet rag, just dampen. Never get a wet rag near an empty socket. Clean the bulbs with ammonia when they are turned off and cooled down. Use

ammonia to clean the chrome on strip lighting as shown above. If the householder smokes, there will accumulate a yellowish-brown layer of smoke on the fixture and the bulbs. Use clear ammonia or Windex each time you clean, to lessen layers of smoke dulling the surface.

Bath scales:

Wipe off bath scales with window cleaner on a rag. Digital scales can be very sensitive to excessive moisture and cause them to quit working properly. Be careful not to move their settings or adjustment knobs when cleaning.

Wastebaskets:

Wipe wastepaper baskets inside and out with an antibacterial cleaner or Clorox Clean-Up. Use a brush and hot soap water for stubborn stuck on dirt. Replace plastic liners, if they use them. Let the client know you store spare bags in the bottom of the basket, so they don't get thrown away by accident. Remove a ceramic wastebasket carefully when it is situated close to the toilet. Bumping it could crack the toilet and the basket.

Tight faucets:

If a single-handled faucet is very hard to turn on, you might mention that the stem or cartridge inside can easily be replaced. This applies to their sink and shower fixtures in the bathroom and kitchen. If the fixture still looks great, the following step could save the homeowner some money, as a plumber might want to replace the whole fixture. This aids you as a cleaner, if they repair this problem, as some handles get very hard to pull up. Elderly people may have difficulties turning on tight faucets.

Pop up the protective cap. Remove the screw to take off the handle. Pull the stem out and put in the replacement. Screw the handle back on and snap the cover back into place. This should solve the problem. The faucet should now turn on with ease, like brand new. If you have any difficulties, talk with the hardware store people, who are usually glad to share their knowledge with you.

The Moen brand faucet stem is held in place by a horseshoe shaped clip. The tool to remove this clip is in the package with the replacement part. Remove the clip, pull up the stem, drop in the new one, and replace the clip and handle. If the hot and cold water comes out in reverse, just remove the clip again, give the replacement stem a half turn, then replace the horseshoe clip and reattach the handle and snap on the cap.

Wash your hands:

Always wash your hands really good with soap after cleaning the bathrooms. Take the time to wash your hands thoroughly so the soap will kill the germs. Rinse well with water. If you use a cleaned sink, again, dry with a clean rag to shine.

Living Room

Some people rarely step into their living room when they have a family room. If so, this area will be easy to keep clean.

Dust first, this way you vacuum up the dust and you're not walking all over the carpet leaving footprints.

Open up the drapes or blinds and turn on lights as needed. Look across the furniture towards the light after you've dusted to see if you missed anything on the wood or glass tables. Carry the furniture polish, window cleaner, and a couple rags to dust and clean any glass. Check any front windows for handprints and smudges. Use Windex or Great Glass Cleaner for glass table tops and for glass sides on any end table. Use a damp cloth to dust a lamp with a brass base, not polish.

Have the caddy handy in the hallway when cleaning the bedrooms, living room, and family room. Use your dry duster first, and then dust the other items with polish. Dust higher up items first: fans, bookshelves, floor lamps, curtain tops, and pictures. This allows time for any dust to settle elsewhere, so you don't have to repeat work. Dust the lamp, the shade on the outside, and up underneath, before dusting the table it sets on.

Neaten the room as you dust. Arrange the pillows on the couch, putting the zipper edges down. Any couch cushions with the zipper in front, turn to the back. Straighten the pictures on the walls, lampshades, stack newspapers, neaten magazines, and untangle phone cords. Prepare the room for vacuuming, moving objects: chairs, baskets, stools, or anything small, all along the edges of the room. These will be the areas you'll vacuum under first. This helps save time when you vacuum.

Move objects to dust under, don't just dust around things. If you slide objects over instead of picking them up, the base usually collects dust that has to be wiped off too. Don't slide any object without felt padding on the bottom across a wood surface. Even picture frames can scratch wood. A heavy lamp with a proper felt pad could be slid without harming anything.

Take your time dusting around their finer objects. A fragile arm could snap off a delicate woman figurine. Pick up those items carefully by the base to prevent breakage.

When using the dry duster, shake the dust off near the floor, then it won't be floating through the air onto the furniture you already dusted. The long-handled duster is good for dusting down coarse wallpaper, or use something like what is pictured below. The duster pictured is a Stanley product.

Furniture polish:

When using furniture polish, use a baby receiving blanket to dust and shine. Cut it in half to make two. Spray close to the rag or direct onto the furniture. Don't let the spray fall towards the carpet. Choose a polish that is easy to use, like Lemon Pledge or Endust, which also leaves a nice lingering scent. Apply polish with one side of the rag and flip it over to shine with the clean side. Dust in the direction of the wood grain. The dustcloth should be washed every time with the rest of the rags.

Use the long-handled nylon duster even on the plain sides of furniture in all the rooms you dust. If you look across the sides towards the light, you will most likely see a light film of clinging dust. Some pieces of furniture may only need polish on the sides two or three times a year. If the furniture has a lot of grooves, it may need a damp brush to eliminate dirt in the cracks. Polish table tops and any areas that are showy.

Some people actually prefer you not to use a lot of furniture polish to avoid build up. Just a light coating of polish will shine most surfaces. The client may request that you dust with a damp cloth. This also keeps the dust from flying around and landing on other pieces of furniture. Some people may request that you not use polish on certain pieces of furniture that are new.

Dust also settles on curved feet of chairs and table legs; use the long duster across them to eliminate a lot of bending down. During the holidays, most clients will tell you not to bother dusting a table loaded with lots of decorations.

Never use furniture polish on a floor, as it would make the floor very slippery and someone could fall. Refer to chapter 3 concerning flooring and carpet.

Dining Room

To dust hanging plates, hold the object with one hand while dusting with the other so that if it does unhook, your chances of an accident are much less. Some people hang delicate objects by a very small nail and sometimes by a large pin, not wanting to put large holes into their nice wallpaper. Pins don't make good anchors. The object is bound to fall someday.

Bookshelves:

Dust the top shelves first and work your way down. Some metal picture frames have rough lower edges that will scratch; carefully pick them up without sliding. Shelves with rows of  many books need to be moved once in a while to clean under. Leaning books will need to be dusted under.

Those who have no sense of arrangement for attractive shelves may appreciate your arranging it for them. Put old magazines and unattractive things in their utility room or garage. Anything important, they will return it to it's proper place. If they don't like their things moved around, they'll tell you.

Piano and organ care:

The following directions are for both organs and pianos. Use a dry duster or a damp cloth to dust. Wood has pores and can plug by being over-polished. Use furniture polish only once or twice a year, but clean the wood surface first with a damp Murphy's Oil Soap cloth to remove the old polish.

Don't spray anything on the keys, it would run down between them and cause internal damage. Use Windex or clear ammonia on a rag to wipe the keys, maybe once or twice a year. This may need to be done more often if frequently used, or if small children are playing with dirty, sticky hands.

Don't move the organ control button settings. Dust the wooden areas, bench, and foot pedals.

Hutches:

You don't usually dust the inside of curio cabinets and hutches that are full of items. If they want you to do it bad enough, they will usually empty it out themselves onto the table and ask you to clean all the glass shelves and doors, inside and out. Use clear ammonia or Great Glass Cleaner with a clean diaper, to ensure no streaking or cloudy appearance. If it has inside lighting, turn it on, as it might help to show any missed spots. They should put the glassware back in themselves.

Chandeliers:

A light fixture above the dining room table can be cleaned with clear ammonia, Great Glass Cleaner, or Windex on the glass parts to avoid streaks and smears. Any brass, or other types of metal, should be wiped with a damp cloth. Clean lightbulbs when they are cold, to prevent breaking the bulbs and getting burned. A very elaborate crystal chandelier might be a project the homeowner cleans themselves, doing so only once a year.

Windowsills:

Dust the windowsills regularly, or use a damp cloth. If they open the windows a lot in the summer, dirt can accumulate quickly, especially if they have any construction taking place in their neighborhood. Some frames and sills get mold growing from moisture. Spray with Clorox Clean-Up, brush, and wipe with a rag, being careful not to get any on the carpeting.

Window tracks:

Clean the window tracks more often in the summer months. Vacuum first with the crevice tool, if needed. You can normally wipe them out with a Windex rag or brush with Clorox Clean-Up if there is a mold problem. Check the patio door tracks each time you clean, as they tend to get a black metal residue that will keep forming when not cleaned regularly. A quick wipe regularly would be easier to maintain. For very stubbron residue, clean with Zud Cleanser and a damp rag.

Glass items:

On glass tabletops, use a good window cleaner and dry with an absorbent cloth or diaper, or use clear ammonia on a clean rag and dry off with another rag. You may need to clean the underneath edges of the glass too. If the table is really heavy with dust, it is easier to dust it off first, and then use the glass cleaner. This causes less streaking and fighting with the dust.

Use a Windex rag to wipe off the tops of picture frames and glass occasionally, and use a duster regularly. Don't spray a glass picture directly. The cleaner should never run down into the frame, it could do some damage. Spray the rag instead.

Glass figurines may need washing with warm soap water, or you can spray them with Windex and rinse. Be very careful with delicate pieces. If the object has a felt bottom, try not to get it wet. Don't set a wet or damp item back onto a wooden table, permanent water marks could develop. These cleaned items may stay nice for a long time, unless it is an unusually dusty house. They will let you know if they have expensive pieces or antiques they would prefer to care for themselves.

Some artificial flower arrangements can be cleaned by spraying with Windex, rinsing with water, and letting drip dry. A large tree can be cleaned outside and hosed down, or you may lean the tree into a shower stall. Don't set a wet tree back on the carpet or on a wooden floor. If you don't want to clean a tree yourself, inform the client of this cleaning method. They will be glad to know they don't have to clean it one leaf at a time.

Cobweb chasing:

Keep a cobweb chaser in the trunk of your car. It would be convenient for you to have the client buy one.

Cobweb chase the following items:

- Everywhere ceilings and walls meet
- Textured ceilings
- Tops of curtains & rods
- Window treatments
- Cold air returns
- Baseboards
- Ceiling beams in family rooms
- Utility rooms
- Exhaust fans
- Light fixture chains
- Ceiling fans and surrounding ceiling
- Behind heavy furniture
- Tops of doors and doorframes
- Baseboard heaters

WEBSTER®
ALL-PURPOSE
DUSTER

Cobweb chase first because the dust falls and settles on everything below. Certain houses have more of a problem and need to be checked more frequently. If dust falls onto the bedspread from the fan, shake the spread, or dust it off. When looking upward while cobweb chasing, be aware of things by your feet to avoid falling over something, like an open dishwasher.

Baseboards:

Run the cobweb chaser along the baseboards if the wood is not too dirty. This can save on your back bending, but at times you may need to use a wet rag with a cleaner, such as Murphy's Oil Soap, or other mild detergents on baseboards. Use a long-handled duster regularly and the wet cloth maybe every 3 to 6 months would be sufficient. Judge each house separately. If they have an aircleaner, dust will be kept at a minimum.

Clean half the baseboards one time and catch the rest next time, if you find it too hard to clean them in one visit. Some vacuums leave black marks on the baseboards. Stubborn marred painted surfaces may need Soft Scrub or Zud to remove nasty black marks. Test a small spot first. Make sure the paint is not fading or coming off. Once you clean these areas try not to cause these marks yourself with the vacuum equipment.

Occasionally use vacuum attachments on carpet areas to get dust clinging around door casings where you can't get close enough with an upright vacuum. Sometimes you can give a quick wipe with a damp cloth or brush to pull the dust away from the wood so it can be cleaned up with the upright vacuum.

Houses with baseboard heat accumulate a lot of dust and cobwebs around those areas. Spiders often like this area. Use a long-handled duster or cobweb chaser, and vacuum once in a while with an attachment. These will need to be cleaned with Spic And Span occasionally. Clean these in the spring.

Foyer

Closet mirror doors across from the main entrance will show every streak when the front door is opened and the light comes in. Make sure those are especially clean before you leave. Clean any small windows around the front door if dirty. Wipe off their doorbell with Clorox Cleanup. Some people seem to never clean them.

Chandeliers that are attached to high ceilings are something you may never have to clean. You may be able to reach across from the stairway to reach a chandelier to lightly knock off cobwebs. Only do this with a plastic bristled chaser, not one made of material that could get hooked on something. Let them care for those that are in very high vaulted ceilings.

Family Room

You will usually find this room needing more attention than a living room. Use vinegar water to remove any mold from wood wall paneling. Check under couch cushions to eliminate crumbs, quick cleaning with the long-handled duster. At times the vacuum might be needed. Any money or coins you find, leave on their table. This is not finder's keepers.

You may need to vacuum couches and chairs often if they have pets shedding. It's best to get out the upholstery attachment to vacuum. For a quick clean, wipe hair off with a damp glove or damp scrub brush.

UPHOLSTERY TOOL

Vacuum accordion pleated lampshades

with the round dusting brush attachment. Make sure the brushes are clean when vacuuming fine cloth lampshades. Be careful using the crevice tool, it may break the pleats. The dusting brush is also good for cleaning furniture with many grooves or heavy glass table tops that have inset edges that collect crumbs. Use the narrow crevice brush for registers and patio door tracks.

DUSTING BRUSH

Run a cobweb chaser across the tops of doors and the woodwork when you're doing the ceiling and other areas. These areas get especially dirty when there is a fireplace used frequently. Wipe around door knobs, doorcasings, and light switches that get handprints or smears.

Many wicker baskets can be cleaned by spraying with Windex, brushing, and rinsing off with warm water. Do not submerge in water. Let the basket drip dry in a sink, or on a towel. Don't put the basket back on a wood surface until completely dry. Set it in front of a fan or use a hair blowdryer to dry it quicker. Use this cleaning method for pine cones also.

Brass and marble:

Dust brass pieces with a dry cloth, or use a damp cloth when necessary. Don't use ammonia, bleach, cleansers, or any other strong cleaner that could cause spotting or pitting.

Marble tables or windowsills may be wiped with a damp cloth or maybe even Windex, depending on the surface. Ask the owner what they prefer to be used on the marble.

Fireplace:

Newer fireplace doors may have special cleaning instructions. Ask what products they use on them. Some require clear water because of a special coating. For inside older doors, clean with Windex and ammonia to eliminate the dark smoke film. Fireplace bricks or stones can be cleaned, vacuumed with the crevice tool attachment, or brushed with a cobweb chaser. Start with the top bricks working your way down. Likely you'll have a mess at the bottom to vacuum up. The owner usually takes care of the ashes

in the fireplace. An old canister vacuum may be kept just for this purpose, or put the ashes in a metal bucket. Only clean up cold ashes. Brass objects by the fireplace may be wiped with a damp cloth.

FREQUENTLY USED
FIREPLACES NEED
MORE ATTENTION

Office or Den

Computers:

Wipe down a laminated computer desk with Windex, if it isn't too loaded down with papers or equipment. The client may wish to care for this themselves. Don't move around a lot of paper work and confuse their arrangement.

Most computer owners have their own computer screen cleaners. Let them care for this. You may want to run a yarn duster across a turned-off screen. Don't spray liquids on the screen that can run down into the edges and cause damage.

Shelves:

Shelves with many books seldom have to be moved to dust. Dust the wood that shows and run a duster across the tops of the books. Remove the books once or twice a year to dust more thoroughly with polish.

Desk:

A desk loaded with many stacks of paper may be in a certain order and the client won't want you disrupting their system. They won't want to be hunting for an important paper that you moved by accident. It's better not to dust the top of the desk. They may specify that you not clean that area or maybe even the whole room. Hairspray quickly removes black marker off wood.

Bedrooms

To avoid carrying a heavy ammonia bottle upstairs, put a little ammonia on a couple rags and place in the caddy. The same could be done for preparing floor cleaning solution. This will lighten your load.

Prepare the room while you dust. Neaten the bed, smoothing the spread, straighten pictures and lampshades, untangle phone cords, and arrange the decorative pillows.

Hold any dresser mirrors with a firm grip when polishing the frame or cleaning the glass, because many mirrors will tilt back, and bump the wall. If you spray the window cleaner directly on the mirror, don't let the liquid run down into the wood area. Spray the window cleaner closer to the top and middle of the mirror. Dry the mirror wiping both directions, sideways and up and down, to eliminate streaks. Use a diaper or very absorbent clean rag and Great Glass Cleaner, to help have a shiny mirror without a cloudy appearance or smears.

A window cleaner bottle left on the dresser could leave a ring or watermark. Don't lay the bottle on a bedspread where it could leak and make a spot. Wipe the tops of perfume bottles on the dresser with a Windex rag and arrange all the bottles orderly, from large to small or in a decorative fashion.

Dressers with many grooves on the trim can be cleaned with a wet brush to get dirt out of the cracks or vacuum out. Every few months you may want to clean these areas more thoroughly. Spray the furniture polish on the rag instead of on the furniture when there are lots of grooves on the top surface, so globs of polish don't get caught in them. Don't slide a piggy bank heavy with coins across wood, it could scratch the furniture because of the weight. When clothing is sticking out of their dresser drawers, open the drawer slightly and shove them back in, otherwise it leaves a sloppy look.

Dust down the chains of any hanging light fixtures with a dry duster. Clean any hanging wall or door mirrors.

Many of the long-handled dusters or cobweb chasers can be bent on the end to make it easy to dust canopy bed rails and ceiling fans. Dust the headboard front and back when it has spindles. Run the long duster behind the nightstand and dressers periodically. These areas often get cobwebs because of floor registers being near. You may want to check the floor behind the headboard once in a while, often feathers and much dust settles there. Use a vacuum attachment to reach this area. Those who have allergies need this area kept very clean. Don't volunteer to change sheets on bunk beds, it's very difficult. Straighten the blankets and comforter quickly when necessary.

If you accidently move controls on their alarm clock, you better leave them a note for them to check it.

Kill spiders on the ceiling with a corn broom. Dust down the door hinges and vacuum the carpeting behind the doors. Pull dust away from carpet around doorstoppers with a damp cloth.

Walk-in closet:

A cold light bulb sprayed with perfume will give off a nice scent when the light is turned on. This is good for a closet that holds odors. People with allergies might not appreciate this, so use this method in your own home only. Hang up empty hangers, belts, or ties that have fallen. Dust across the clothing hanger rod occasionally, and across shoes that tend to never get worn, they can get quite dusty. Pair and neaten the shoes.

Baby Nursery

Baby cribs on wheels can be easily moved to vacuum under. Wipe the edge of the crib with something to kill germs, and then rinse with a wet rag. Straighten the blankets and stuffed animals in the crib. Make sure your hands are clean before handling an infant's crib area.

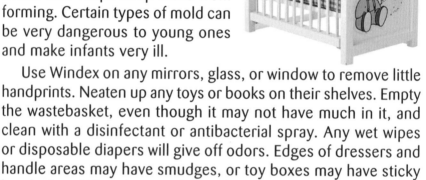

Check window edges and the windowsills regularly to make sure mold is not growing. Clean any mold growth with Clorox Clean-Up, which also helps keep more from forming. Certain types of mold can be very dangerous to young ones and make infants very ill.

Use Windex on any mirrors, glass, or window to remove little handprints. Neaten up any toys or books on their shelves. Empty the wastebasket, even though it may not have much in it, and clean with a disinfectant or antibacterial spray. Any wet wipes or disposable diapers will give off odors. Edges of dressers and handle areas may have smudges, or toy boxes may have sticky handprints. Wipe these with Windex or antibacterial sprays.

A young person's bedroom may need a little added touch of

straightening. They may have extra toys, or older youth have gadgets and collectibles to arrange or put in the closet on shelves. Use Clorox Clean-Up on light switch plates. Clean the dressers with the appropriate cleaner as suggested in the last section on bedrooms. Children's white laminated furniture is easily cleaned by wiping with Windex to remove handprints and bring out the shine.

Utility Room

Door handles going into the garage usually get very dirty. Be sure to wipe this area and the light switch plate. Check the automatic garage door opener button and clean it every few months. This usually gets totally neglected.

Wipe down the washer and dryer with Windex, even lifting the washer lid occasionally and wiping the edges on the inside where soap and dirt collect. That's one of those extras your client will appreciate.

If you move their clothes dryer while wiping up the floor, don't push the dryer too close to the back wall. When air vents get twisted or blocked, they will automatically turn the heat off while running. This is a safety measure to prevent fires. If that happens your client might call a repairman unnecessarily, which would be costly for a service call.

Some people have their dryer vents hooked in an unsafe manner. You certainly don't want this to fall off and have to go through the hassle to put it back on. It's better not to move the dryer to begin with.

The long-handled nylon duster can be used to pull dust out from between the two appliances, if it's not too dirty. You could also use a vacuum attachment or run a yardstick underneath to pull out excess dirt. Dryer lint gets the floor really dusty and many objects often roll under the appliances.

If the furnace and hot water tank are in this room also, the top of the hot water tank will accumulate a lot of dust. Quickly dust it off with a dry duster. If they are in a closet, you don't clean them. Let them take care of that area.

Utility tubs:

Fiberglass utility tubs clean well with Soft Scrub containing bleach, Comet, or Clorox Clean-Up. For unusual stubborn stains, you could apply Lime-A-Way. Let it set for a few minutes, and then scrub with a nylon scratch pad. Use your window razor or butter knife to scrape off any paint drippings. Be careful not to cut the surface of the fiberglass.

Spray Lime-A-Way around the faucet and brush away the dirt, but make sure you don't mix a bleach product with these. Rinse with plenty of water. When the faucet fixture is very close to the wall, use the narrow grout brush. If that doesn't fit, use an old toothbrush, or seesaw a rag through the area. If you use Clorox Clean-Up to clean the tub, again, rinse well, so any clothes thrown into the wet sink later won't get bleached spots and be ruined.

Some washing machines have the drain hose that will be looped over the utility sink, so clean the drain of any lint that might be slowing the water drainage. Don't leave a rag in the sink, it could block the drain and the water will overflow onto the floor when they do their laundry. Put the dirty rags in a bucket. Clean off any soap dishes, soap dispensers, and even the bar of soap can be cleaned lightly with a brush.

If you are dumping buckets of dirty water in the utility tub, you might as well clean it last. Very dirty water should be flushed down the toilet or dumped outside to avoid clogging the drain.

Utility rooms in each house can vary drastically in needs. Some will have a lot of items stacked and stored. You are not required to move such things. Just a quick cleaning in the utility room is usually all that is required. Clean the floor.

Concrete utility tubs are usually in the basement, an area you won't be cleaning.

Chapter 3

Flooring

Linoleum

Before cleaning a kitchen floor, sweep up the loose dirt with a broom and dustpan. Use an angled broom with the bristle edges that are split because they are very good at sweeping up fine particles. Clean down basement stairways that are not closed off by a door. It helps keep the main house cleaner.

Don't use an upright vacuum with rotating brushes on a linoleum floor, as it could grind holes into a softer linoleum. There are many upright vacuums made specifically for bare floors, without rotating brushes, such as the one pictured here.

RICCAR®
OMNI

No wax floor

A no-wax floor needs very little cleaning solution. Some prefer to use cleaners made particularly for no-wax floors. Don't use liquid or dry cleanser on a shiny no-wax floor; it could ruin the floor and leave dull spots.

A few drops of Spic And Span and two or three tablespoons of clear ammonia in a small bucket of water will usually clean the floor nicely, leaving it streak-free. To get this small amount of a liquid cleaner, turn the bottle upside down while still capped, turn back upright, and remove the lid and rinse the lid into the bucket of water. This way you get a little soap without dumping too much in the bucket by mistake and it's quicker to prepare the bucket.

Too much soap will cause a streaky film and stickiness. If the floor is sticky, you used too much soap or there is some type of wax on it that the ammonia may have softened. Don't use ammonia on a waxed floor unless you're stripping it.

An exceptionally dirty or older floor may require more soap than a new floor. Some may have layers of wax on a no-wax floor to acquire more of a shine. With improper cleaning over a period of time, dirt is waxed into indentations in the floor.

Clean layers of wax off with strong soap and ammonia, or stripping solution. Use a long-handled brush, such as the Swivel Scrub, and finish up with a hand scrub brush to do the greater detail close to cabinets and baseboards. Be sure to have your kneeling pads on. When the floor is cleaned properly, it may shine once again. If this doesn't work, try using Mop & Glo. This product is easier to remove than a regular floor wax.

Some floors merit your getting down on your hands and knees to clean properly. Even when using the sponge mop, you still need to clean around the sink cabinet edges with a rag in order to get close to the cabinets.

Don't leave excess water lying on tiles or linoleum that has unsealed seams. The water could run under the seams and cause spots on tiles or linoleum to loosen or buckle up.

A floor that has not been taken care of regularly, may have dirt sealed into many coats of wax. Refer to the next page on stripping wax for more detail.

Some chair legs collect dirt on the bottom or on their rollers and knobs that make ugly dirt spots on the floor. You need to clean these periodically.

Removing scuff marks:

Scuff marks or tar spots made by shoes can be removed from a no-wax floor with Goo Gone. It leaves a slickness of oil, so you have to clean that off with regular floor cleaner. If you forget, someone could fall. An older floor that will absolutely not clean up with the usual method may need stronger cleaners. Test out a spot with Clorox Clean-Up or Soft Scrub. Make sure it's not dulling the surface. These should only be used as a last resort on an older no-wax floor, where marks won't come off.

Commercial type vinyl tile that has scuff marks on it can be hard work to clean up. Try stepping onto two pot scrubbing pads, scooting your feet across the floor to clean large areas. Keep in mind this might scratch a floor that has wax on it. If you clean that type of floor, perhaps even their basement, you should charge extra!

Waxed Floors

If washing a heavily waxed floor, use a mild soap or a little Spic And Span. Don't put any ammonia in the water unless you plan on stripping the wax off. It would start to remove the wax, making the floor sticky, and then you'll have to strip it. Always clean the floor before adding another layer of wax.

Stripping a waxed floor:

The owner might be surprised to find they still have a nice floor under all that wax build up, but never had anyone to clean the floor properly. Perhaps it won't need wax at all. Some old floors may never clean up to look good again. Just do the best you can. They will probably replace the floor anyway.

If this is going to be a major undertaking to remove, you want to be paid extra for this, or make it the only thing you clean that day. You'll probably use muscles you haven't used in a while if the floor is really heavily waxed. If you're not using an electric scrubber on a larger floor, you will be sore.

Use a long-handled brush, the Swivel Scrub, or a deck brush for the initial stripping, if you don't have an electric scrubber. Get on your hands and knees to do the final scrubbing, and use a good stiff bristled brush. Wear your kneeling pads. Test a couple areas to see what product will work best.

Floor stripping cleaners and equipment:
- Strong ammonia with Spic And Span (or other floor product)
- Wax-stripping products
- Commercial cleaners (buy at janitorial store)
- Electric floor scrubber
- Large towel rags and a bucket
- Butter knife, plastic putty knife, or plastic scraper
- Nylon mesh scrubber with handle
- Stiff bristled brush
- Heavy duty gloves
- Swivel Scrub with long handle
- Floor fan
- Breathing mask

If there is good weather outside, open the windows and use a floor fan to have plenty of air movement. You don't want to be overcome by fumes if you are using ammonia. If the fumes are too strong, add more water to the solution or wear a breathing mask of some sort.

Apply the stripping solution. Let it set about five minutes  while you're preparing the next area to allow the product time to soften the wax, then come back and start scrubbing. Repeat this procedure for heavily waxed floors until clean. Rinse with cold water, and dry with large towel rags. Avoid water leaking into loose floor seams, causing damage.

Dump the dirty water down the toilet and flush immediately to keep the toilet clean.

If the owner has a septic tank, they will prefer you to dump the water outside where it won't cause any problems. They might instruct you on that matter.

Applying floor wax:

When cleaning the room, prepare for the floor waxing by removing the wastebasket, chairs, and other small items.

Mop & Glo type products may be used on a floor that have a dull finish. Clean the floor first, and then apply the Mop & Glo to acquire a shine. Apply the solution with a damp cloth and overlapping strokes so there won't be any missed streaks on the floor. Touch up any missed spots that would be obvious. Make application so you can exit the room.

Apply Future Floor Finish only when the floor is clean so you're not sealing dirt into the floor. Apply a thin coat of wax with a wax applicator or use a damp cloth. Repeat another thin layer when dry, if necessary. Never try to put another application on when the floor is still tacky. When applying more wax on another visit, always clean the floor first with a mild soap. Many layers of wax can make a floor very shiny. Never leave a puddle of water on the wax, it could cause a white filmy spot to remain.

Allow enough time for drying so you can put the furniture back before leaving. If not, let them return the chairs later. They won't want the chairs stuck to the floor, causing ugly marks. Don't get wax on table legs or the wall baseboards. Don't wax up to the cabinets. Leave an inch or two unwaxed, because this will make it easier to strip in the future. Rinse the waxing rag thoroughly before putting it in with the laundry rags. Also, rinse the wax applicator so it won't harden.

Many are replacing old floors with easy care floors that can often be damp mopped.

Ceramic Tile

Ceramic tile floors are usually sealed and can be wiped with clear water, especially a newer floor. Vacuum the tile with a floor attachment to get loose dirt out of the grout areas and then mop. If you don't vacuum the tile first, dirt in the grout area can turn into mud and will need to be scrubbed out.

For a smaller floor, clean with the wet rag and follow with a dry rag. Wear your kneeling pads or kneel on a folded towel rag. Some tile can be wiped up with just a little ammonia added to the water, one or two tablespoons. For larger areas you may want to use a sponge mop or rag mop. Large floors with very little dirt and a smooth surface wipe up very nice with the Star Fiber Mop by slightly dampening the pad.

When cleaning a kitchen floor, be sure to wipe under the cabinets with a rag first as some mops can't get close enough to do a good job. These areas tend to collect crumbs.

Tile with white grout that has become dark can be sprayed with Clorox Clean-Up. Let set 5 or 10 minutes, then scrub with a stiff brush. Repeat, if necessary. Rinse thoroughly because bleach products will make a sponge mop crumble. The owner may want to seal the tile again. After that, clean with clear water or a little ammonia added to the water. This will cut enough of the dirt without leaving streaks or stickiness on the floor. If it leaves a soap film or is sticky, you know you put too much cleaner in the water. Rinse the floor with clear cold water and dry with a towel rag to solve the problem. Don't leave the floor tacky.

A broken ceramic tile in a main room or hallway can ruin a neat appearance. If the owner has no spare tiles, suggest one could be removed from a closet or hidden spot to replace the damaged one that shows.

Light colored grout can be easily stained to a darker color. This could be suggested to the homeowner when the grout has become unsightly. There are colored grout stains that can be bought in a pint or quart. The stain is applied to the grout and then wiped off the tile. If the tile is in very good shape, the staining will make it look new again.

Hardwood Floors

You may need to use a dust mop on wooden floors. Some older floors may be fine with a dampened mop, while other newer wooden floors will need special cleaners. A hardwood floor that has not been taken care of can be cleaned with

Murphy's Oil Soap. Some might request the cleaner to use ammonia, clear water, vinegar water, or no water at all. If it is a newer floor, the owner was probably informed as to the type of cleaner to be used on that specific floor when it was installed.

The Starfiber Mop pictured here, is great for smooth large area tile, hardwood floors, and linoleum. It comes with washable cloth pads that you can use dry or dampened. You can mop first with the wet pad and then change to a dry pad to remove any moisture or streaking. It's a great product!

The Swiffer Mop is great for a quick spruce up of small floors. The thin throw away sheet attracts fine dirt and hair. The mop can be stored easily because of its size and can also be purchased with a wider base. These are great for the times you don't feel like pulling out the mop, bucket, and soap.

Never leave any excess water on a wooden floor that could leak into seams and cause buckling or loosening of the flooring. Quick dry with a large towel rag.

When dry mopping, dust under dressers and beds when possible. Use the long duster to reach under furniture that has very short legs where the mop won't fit, or use a vacuum attachment. Some of the newer floors have protective coatings or laminates that make it possible to slide furniture without scratching. Check with the homeowner.

SWIFFER®
MOP

Carpeting

To spot-clean carpeting, vacuum the carpet first, if dry. Brush up spots of dirt with clear ammonia and water on a rag. Wipe using a dry light towel rag, rubbing the dirt onto the towel. Brush up the nap of the carpet, and let it dry before vacuuming again. Products that leave detergent on the carpet will attract dirt to that area again. Soap on carpeting can be removed by steam cleaning.

DL Hand Cleaner for mechanics is a lanoline used without water and will remove grease, gum, and oily substances from material, but afterward, remove the odor with clear ammonia. Always test cleaner on a small inconspicuous spot first.

DL HAND CLEANER
PURCHASE IN
AUTOMOTIVE SECTION

Don't clean large areas of carpet. Carpet cleaning is a big job and is usually left for the owners. They may hire professionals or rent the proper machines to clean it themselves.

Never use bleach to clean a spot on carpeting, even a light colored carpet would discolor. If there is a bleach spot or stain on the surface of a long-napped carpet, it might be possible to trim the tips off to remove the worst of the spot.

Sparks from a fireplace with just a surface burn could be slightly trimmed. A burned hole can be fixed by trimming a little carpet from an edge or closet somewhere and mixing the fragments with a little glue to repair. This is something you could try on your own carpet.

A ruined spot of carpet can also be replaced. If the owner didn't keep a spare piece of carpet when it was installed, a square could be cut from a closet or underneath a piece of furniture that never gets moved. The patch may not show at all, depending on the nap of the carpet. Have a professional carpet layer make this repair, as they have the proper equipment and adhesives to do this. If you see a ruined spot on a client's carpet, you might suggest this little trick.

Vacuuming

Vacuum the carpet in the direction that makes the nap of the carpet look the best. Try a couple directions. There are usually height settings on the vacuum for the different types of carpet. Try the lower setting to see if it cleans and looks better. The lower settings tend to pick up the nap better and may help a problem area.

When dusting, prepare the rooms for vacuuming as you work along. Move small chairs, magazine racks, plants, baskets, or anything small around the edges. Vacuum under those areas first and then vacuum the main traffic area last.

When vacuuming underneath a table holding a lamp, pull up the lamp cord above the table first so the rotator brush won't catch the cord. When vacuuming an area rug on a wooden floor, don't damage the floor with the rotator brush.

Areas near a patio door or high volume walk area may have more sandy dirt that needs to be vacuumed over several times. If you continue to hear sand flying up the vacuum, move the vacuum slower.

Some vacuums have at least one side as an edger. Run the vacuum close to the baseboards, trying not to scrape or harm the woodwork. Loosen any lint or stuck particles with your fingers

and vacuum up. Pace the speed of your vacuuming to allow enough time to suck up dirt and lint.

If you vacuum up one strip of carpet, return pulling backwards on the same strip. The backward stroke picks up the most dirt and leaves the carpeting looking attractive. You have actually vacuumed that area twice. Slightly overlap each strip, to leave less carpet marks. Vacuum with the cord over your shoulder and excess cord behind you. The cord is in danger of getting ran over, as shown in the picture. Try to vacuum out of a room and not walk on the carpet again. Some clients won't walk into their living room for days to prolong that great look!

Never vacuum over wet carpeting from an over-watered plant, pet urine, or spot cleaning. When you clean a carpet spot, vacuum it first, clean, and then lift up the carpet nap with a scrub brush. Don't vacuum again until it's dry, because any dirt from the rotator brushes will go onto the carpeting.

Don't try to move heavy furniture to vacuum. You don't want to strain your back, nor will the homeowner want you getting hurt at their house. There are many smaller pieces of furniture that you can probably move part of the time.

Vacuum carpeted steps with your upright vacuum for better suction. If that's not possible, perhaps the homeowner has an electric hand-held vacuum with a rotating brush, as the one pictured.

Vacuum under beds occasionally. If a lot of items are stored under the bed, don't bother. Some vacuums will collapse flat enough to go under bed frames that have higher side rails. If not, use a vacuum attachment. Dust accumulates behind

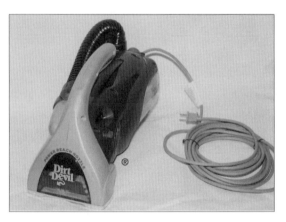

headboards and on the baseboards. There may be a register against the wall in that area, and forced air heating will cause a lot of cobwebs and dust to accumulate. Pillows and blankets produce a lot of lint.

Vacuum a walk-in closet each time you clean and other closets as needed. You normally don't have to move the shoes, but occasionally this could be done in a walk-in closet. Match the shoes and put them back in an orderly fashion. If they have many pairs of shoes, you won't be inclined to do this. Hang up any empty hangers, belts, or ties that have fallen. Dust any open shelves in the closet and clean any wall mirrors. Now the closet is ready to vacuum.

Also check their hallway linen and coat closets and vacuum into these once in a while.

Don't vacuum up red poinsettia leaves, the rotator brush may smear the color onto the carpet. Pick up any dead leaves in or out of the pot and throw them in the garbage.

Avoid vacuuming up any objects that may get trapped in your vacuum cleaner. The internal fans can freeze-up with something stuck in them, needing expensive repair. String can wrap around the rotating brushes, belts can stretch or break when caught on rugs.

Don't vacuum up these objects:

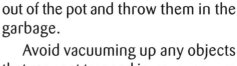

- Coins
- String or yarn
- Christmas tree tinsel
- Easter basket grass
- Blind strings
- Cords to computers
- Extension cords
- Lamp cords
- Dust ruffles on beds
- Edge of bedspreads
- Electric blanket cords
- Edges of rugs & fringe
- Small toys
- Shoelaces
- Rubberbands
- Paper clips
- Window treatment that drapes on the floor
- Small chains hanging from vertical slats
- Phone cords

If you pull the cord out of the outlet from a distance to avoid walking on the vacuumed area, make sure it's straight on, so the cord doesn't swing around and break or scatch something. With some cords you can't do this without damaging the plug. If you do this with an extension cord, you can always replace it after a period of time. Most new vacuums are now made with sturdier plugs and longer cords which are more convenient.

Various pieces of furniture may not have solid wood down to the floor and so dust will accumulate underneath between the legs where the upright vacuum can't reach. You may need to use the vacuum attachments. You can also pull up the carpet nap with a long-handled deck brush in hard to reach areas, or with a scrub brush.

A house that doesn't have enough electrical outlets in hallways can be annoying when you have to replug into every room. You may want to attach a 10-15 foot extension cord to avoid this problem. If the extension cord is too long or too heavy, you'll find yourself fighting a tangled cord or having trouble keeping it out of the way, defeating the purpose of convenience.

Always have the vacuum in the 'off' position when plugging it in, and have it setting on carpeting in case it was accidently bumped on. Don't unplug anything that is important or that has clock settings to plug in the vacuum. Look for another outlet. Sometimes you can plug into the bathroom that is off the hallway in order to vacuum the nearby bedrooms.

Don't leave the vacuum setting upright, with the switch turned on and the brushes rotating. It could make dirt streaks on the carpeting, especially if the roller brush is starting to get dirty.

Vacuum slower when near furniture legs or around leather furniture. Bumping them may put a tear in the leather or scratches on the wood. Touch-up your own furniture with a stain polyurethane. Keep a small can on hand for accidental nicks.

When preparing a child's room for vacuuming, pick up toys and put them into the toy box, or on any shelves used to store toys. Stuffed animals usually go on the bed. Neaten the room before vacuuming.

Vacuum first in the areas where the small items have been moved around the edges of the rooms and then do the main part of the room, vacuuming out of the room. Don't walk back on the carpet unless absolutely necessary. Your client will enjoy seeing the carpeting without any footprints on it.

Some vacuums will automatically shut off when something gets caught in the brush, like the edge of a rug. This prevents further damage to the item and also protects the vacuum. Pull the item out from the brush assembly and turn the vacuum back on. It if won't start, it may have a restart button. It's often red and on the lower back base of the vacuum.

Throw rugs will need shaking by each end. Shake outside if possible. Don't shake near furniture or there will be dust floating through the air. Some vacuums have a lower speed for using on more delicate rugs. Use it when vacuuming a firmer type throw rug, especially when they have fringe of some type on the ends. A powerful vacuum may pull the ends off and leave an unsightly looking edge. Even plain-edged rugs getting caught will ruin their rubber backing and cause crumbling. Always click the vacuum off as quick as you can when something gets caught. When the belts are stretched, the brush assembly won't be turning as good, and dirt pickup will lessen.

Be careful when vacuuming around breakable objects, large ceramic statues, or plant pots that can chip or crack. Pick up dead leaves and put them into a wastebasket. Sometimes people over water their plants and the excess overflows onto the carpet.

Some clients like to sprinkle a powder product on their carpeting to eliminate odors. Some types can gum up the internal parts of the vacuum and then it will need to be cleaned out by a repairman. Ask your client not to use these products if you're using your own vacuum. If they insist on using them, then use their vacuum instead of yours.

Those who have pets tend to be the ones who use these products. Be alert to their use, because the householder may sprinkle these products on the carpet before you come to clean. You might smell it when you enter the room.

If you use their vacuum all the time, it would be better to have your own vacuum in the trunk as a back-up, in the event theirs quits working, or their belts break and you can't find the replacements. Ask where they store the spare bags and belts.

Chapter 4

Windows & Doors

Window Treatments

Mini blinds sometimes will have a strip at the top side that will easily fall down when touched with the cobweb chaser or cleaning with a rag. Be careful not to knock them off and then have to reassemble parts. Regularly dust down mini-blinds, otherwise, they get very dirty. Shut the blinds with the rounded slats downward, this is the side that usually gets most of the dust. The long nylon duster or yarn duster is really good for this job. If the cord is very tight when closing large slat blinds, don't force them to move. Let the homeowner figure out the problem so you don't make it worse.

Mini-blinds can be cleaned with a clear ammonia rag. This takes a little time if you're not in a hurry that day. Very dirty blinds can be laid down in a bathtub and cleaned with Spic And Span and ammonia in the water. Rinse well. It actually isn't good to get any metal parts at the top wet, they could rust. Check first to see if most of the parts are plastic.

With modern decorating, you will see different kinds of window treatments rather than standard drapes on traverse rods. Many use material elegantly draped around rods and flowing down to the floor. You may see material decoratively put on a permanent large valance base like the one shown above. These can be vacuumed off with an attachment periodically and dusted with the long nylon duster regularly. Run the cobweb chaser along the very top to knock down dust. Curtain tieback brackets stick out from the wall several inches. If you bump them they can break.

Windows

Some housecleaners will not clean windows. It would be wise to do some regularly that are often used and have handprints, such as patio doors or the front storm door. Choose the most absorbent clean rags for this job. It may be easy to do some of the inside windows part of the time as needed. The client may pay you an extra $10-$20 to clean both the inside and outside.

Clean inside the windows first, and then clean the outside. If a screen is stuck and can't be removed, open the window enough that you can clean both sides from the outside. Take a safe ladder or a stepstool with you outside so you can reach the top edge of the window. Be careful not to step on sprinkler systems in landscaped flowerbeds. Decorative window pane dividers will be in between the panes of glass, those that aren't, be careful removing to avoid breaking.

Many newer windows can be cleaned on both sides from the inside of the house. Open the window upward a couple inches; put a large spool of thread (same size) under each side of the opened window. Move the release buttons at the top of the bottom glass section. Slowly tilt the window down towards you, keeping the sides that connect evenly balanced on the spools. This hopefully will prevent parts from springing out of place in the sidetracks. If your client knows they have a problem with the side rails popping out, they should make you aware of this. You can inform them of this spool method to help them. Windows in very good condition will not need the spools.

Windows often have paint and sap spots that need to be scraped off with a safety glass scraper. Use the retractable razor so you can carry it in your pocket when cleaning the outside windows. Clean the long narrow windows next to their front door entrance, as they get smudges from dogs and toddlers little handprints. Unhealthy or elderly people can get by using a long-handled squeegee to clean their own windows.

Some homes have a lot of glass throughout the house. If you have a client that has a great deal of glass to clean, it may be advantageous to have an industrial strength window cleaner that is streak free. The product shown is appropriately named, Great Glass Cleaner. It comes in an aerosol can, it cleans great, smells wonderful, and is reasonably priced. It is sold by the case of 12 or 24. You might want to split a case with a friend or relative to reduce the cost. There will also be a shipping and handling fee.

GREAT GLASS CLEANER®
MADE BY:
CCP INDUSTRIES®
P.O. BOX 6500
CLEVELAND, OH
1-800-321-2840

Doors

Interior doors:

Inside wooden doors may be wiped down with Murphy's Oil Soap or other cleaners made for wood. Very dry wood may need something like Holloway House Lemon Oil.

Windex can be used on white painted surface doors to leave them streak free. For more stubborn stains try Clorox Clean-Up, but rinse off. Occasionally clean wooden louver doors with a wet rag wrapped around a butter knife or putty knife, it helps to get closer to the side edges. On metal doors, use water or Windex, and dust regularly thereafter.

Patio doors:

Patio door tracks get an ugly black muck that forms from the movement of parts across the metal. Vacuum out loose dirt first, then spray the track with Clorox Clean-Up and clean with a brush and rag, then rinse. Use Zud for an exceptionally dirty

track. Regular wiping with a wet rag may be sufficient.

When you're cleaning the outside glass of the door, be sure not to lock yourself out. Some doors will automatically lock when you shut them. To be safe, you could toss something across the track, like the handle of a duster or a rag so the door can't shut. Don't leave the patio door open while cleaning the outside glass. Just crack the door a little, because a chipmunk or squirrel could run into the house, or a pet could sneak out, then you'd have to retrieve it.

Entrance doors:

Always clean the front storm door and patio door inside and out, if weather permits. If they have a dog, there will always be messes on both sides of the glass. Often the door they use the most will be the one accessing through the garage. It will accumulate a lot of marks and dirty handprints. Clean the door handles, the glass, wipe the threshold, and sometimes the metal parts on the inside of the storm door. If they have a mat just outside the entrance, shake off dirt and leaves to keep them from getting tracked into the house.

Clean the front doorbell with Clorox Clean-Up or a disinfectant, maybe once or twice a year. Many people never think to check this.

Beware of a cat or dog who might slip out the door when you open it. You don't want to be chasing an animal down the street.

Screens:

Screens on patio doors or windows can be wiped down with a duster or lightly wiped with a very wet ammonia rag. The rag will turn black with dirt. Don't press hard to avoid pulling the screen out of its edges. This is a quick method for those times when you can't pull all the screens out to clean more thoroughly. Cleaning all the screens is not a normal duty for a housecleaner, but a spring cleaning type project for the homeowner.

If you wear tennis shoes while cleaning, make sure you keep the bottoms clean. When stepping outside to clean the patio doors or windows, you may have to step onto mulch or flowerbeds. Have a rag to clean off your shoes before entering back into the house, or take off your shoes and clean them. Let them dry before walking around on the clean floors.

Chapter 5

What To Clean

Special or Unusal Items

Piano or organ:

Don't use polish on a piano or organ unless the client asks you to. Dust with a damp cloth or nylon duster. Don't spray anything on the keyboard, as the liquid would run down inside and cause some damage. Spray the cloth with Windex or dampen with ammonia and wipe the keys.

Marble and stone:

Wipe with a damp cloth or with a little Windex. There are now many surfaces such as Corian and stones that are quite durable and used as kitchen countertops. Wipe these with Windex to shine.

Brass:

Brass lamps, beds, candlesticks, frames, and other items need to be dusted with a dry cloth, or a damp cloth when necessary. There are brass and metal cleaners for those older items that won't clean up by any simple method.

Silver:

There are many creme type products on the market to clean silver objects that make it a simple task. Regular dusting and occasional cleaning with cremes would be sufficient.

Computers:

Dust off computer screens only when turned off. Let them take care of the regular cleaning with their own screen cleaner sprays. Be careful not to mess with your client's computer. You certainly wouldn't want to accidentally break or delete anything important. Don't vacuum near any cords that are under the computer desk and get any cords caught in the rotator brush.

Harp:

Clean a harp with a damp cloth, if they instruct you to do so.

A harp is a very fine instrument, therefore, you need to take care that you don't scratch or mar it in some way. They may just tell you not to bother with it at all. Likely they will want to care for this item themselves.

Oil paintings:

Dust down lightly with the long duster. Don't spray any cleaners on an oil painting. Wipe the frame with a damp cloth occassionally. A freshly painted oil portrait will take a long time to dry, perhaps even a year. Don't touch the surface of the portrait until the client lets you know it's safe to do so. Dust the frame with a damp cloth to avoid dust landing on the painting.

Stairway railings:

Use a damp cloth with a little Murphy's Oil Soap to remove any grime or handprints. Use a little polish only once or twice a year to prevent wax build up.

Leather furniture:

You could suggest that they clean their own leather furniture with cleaner made for that purpose. Other types of cleaners can cause damage to leather furniture. Vinyl is different from leather, and

can be wiped with other cleaners. Some vinyl will shine up nicely with furniture polish. Before you use anything, ask the client if they have a personal preference.

Accordion lampshades:

This type lampshade can be vacuumed with the crevice tool as shown below, or you can use the dusting brush attachment to get the dust out of the narrow grooves. Don't force the crevice tool too far into the pleats, as it may damage them.

LAMP WITH ACCORDION SHADE

CREVICE TOOL

Chalk board:

A chalk board can be wiped with a wet cloth. Use a citrus cleaner, Goo Gone, or Orange Clean to remove crayon marks.

Fish tanks:

Wipe off the glass around the outside of a fish tank. Little handprints smear the glass when there are children in the house.

Bedspread:

If a wrinkled comforter is a cotton/polyester fabric, it could possibly be pressed right on the bed, but only if it is clean. Hook an extension cord to the iron, and press with steam on a *low* heat. Keep the iron moving or you could burn it because the stuffing to a comforter will hold the heat. To be on the safe side, test a small spot on the underside first. Don't try this on delicate fabrics; dry clean instead. Don't try this on cleaning jobs.

Pictures:

Plastic picture frames can be wiped down with Windex. The picture shown here has vertical plastic grooves and needs only to be cleaned with Windex or dusted.

Antiques & collectibles:

The client might have a collection as the one pictured here. They may prefer caring for these items themselves, especially for those that are irreplaceable, precious to them, or costly. Don't use soaps, hot water, or soak antiques in water to prevent cloudy appearance or color fading.

Shelves:

Move items on shelves to dust and wipe glass items off with Windex to make them shine. Don't just dust around objects; move them, or dust will show when sunlight shines across them. Be careful with anything that is fragile.

Televisions:

Wipe a standard television screen with Windex, never letting the solution run down into the bottom edge. If a solution would get into the electrical components, this could cause a short, and perhaps a fire. Spray the rag, then wipe. Move any tapes laying near and dust the cabinet.

A television hung on the wall can be easily dusted with the long nylon duster. Don't clean projection screens because they need special attention. Let the homeowner care for this.

Metal items:

Metal tables may only need to be wiped down with a damp cloth and plain water, then dried completely. Don't let puddles of water lie on the surface, because any breaks in the protective coating will allow water to seep in and form a permanent spot. Wipe the rungs and vinyl seats of the chairs with Windex. On a regular basis just a quick dusting on the rungs will be sufficient.

Light fixture:

Regular dusting with a dry duster will keep something like this light fixture fairly clean. The glass on the chandelier will need Windex occasionally, and the metal parts wiped with a damp cloth.

Wicker:

Use a dry duster on wicker, and clean with a wet rag when spots accumulate. Spray the rag with a little Windex. Some wicker can be cleaned outside, brushed with a soap solution and hosed down. Dry with a towel and let set in the sun to finish drying. This might be a good project to do on a breezy day to expedite drying.

Area rug:

Be careful when vacuuming an area rug so the vacuum's rotator brushes don't touch onto the hardwood floor and cause damage. As you vacuum off near the edges of the rug, tip the vacuum handle down to raise up the brushes off the floor, then roll back up on the rug for the next strip.

Grandfather clock:

Care for the outside of the grandfather clock by dusting with a damp cloth and very little polish on the wood. Use Great Glass Cleaner or clear ammonia on the glass to attain a streak-free

shine. The glass door will need cleaning in and out. The homeowner should clean the inside of the clock themselves a couple times a year, using the dusting brush vacuum attachment to clean the bottom.

Telescope:

A telescope can be lightly dusted off with the nylon or yarn dry duster. Don't get the fibers of the duster caught on any of the intricate little parts or near the fragile viewing end. Be careful to never knock this over, as the lenses or

other parts are delicate.

The client may just simply instruct you to never touch it. Some telescopes are very large and expensive. They may want to take care of this costly item themselves.

Doing Extras

Doing some extras is helpful in keeping the client happy. You might clean something they would never have thought to do. They may keep you cleaning for many years if you are really helpful to them. Remember, if you don't clean something now and you clean for a person every other week, then it will be a month before that item gets cleaned again. You have to decide what things need a regular cleaning and what things should be cleaned occasionally. The owner may not notice you cleaned a certain thing, but if you don't clean it, they are most likely to see that you didn't.

Detail Work

Use a brush around the base of the toilet and cabinets. Clean the floor close up to kitchen cabinets where crumbs collect. Clean around the wastebasket, floor, wall, or inside under the sink.

Wipe around light switch plates, wall plugs, and door handles with Windex, Clorox Clean-Up, or antibacterial cleaners.

Wipe handprints off woodwork, especially near a garage door entrance, patio doors, closets, or children's bedroom doorways.

Clean corners behind doors that collect dust and cobwebs. Use a damp cloth on the hinges and around doorstoppers. Clean into seams around range counters, backsplash of kitchen and bathroom countertops.

Wipe the top edges of range doors. Clean refrigerator tops, the base front inside, and both sides of the handles. Clean the rubber seals around the door when needed.

Use brushes to clean around window and door tracks, and windowsills to keep down mold and dirt.

Vacuum and wipe coat closet floors and around the baseboards. Check under couch and chair cushions, and move small items to vacuum under.

Wipe off perfume bottles, soap dispensers, and any other bottles and things that set out that accumulate dust.

Occasional Clean Items

There are certain things you will always be expected to clean. You have to decide on the things that will be extras and cleaned just occasionally. I make many suggestions, but you will have to decide what's more important for each house. Specific needs will vary from house to house.

Occasionally clean more thoroughly

- Light fixtures
- Ceiling fans
- Registers
- Cold air returns
- Books on shelves
- Glass figurines
- Doors and tops of doors
- Door frames
- Baseboards
- Under beds
- Piano keys
- Under couch cushions
- Upholstery
- Cobwebs
- Phones
- Electric switch plates
- Refrigerator top
- Glass lamps
- Scrolled edges of furniture
- Under shoes in closet
- Coat closet floor
- Closet hanging poles
- Doorbells
- Fingerprints around garage door opener
- Closet shelves
- Outside doorknob into garage from utility room

Vacuum into registers your first or second time in, to keep down dust and cobwebs. Some people may have never done this. You may even find constuction debris still in the ductwork. This is something you don't have to do, but it will help lessen your work. Some houses get lots of crumbs down the registers, especially in the kitchen or near the patio doors. Clean a wall register with a wet brush and dry off to avoid rust.

Cleaning the inside of the toilet tank helps keep the bowl cleaner. It eliminates the accumlating of many rings and the dark lines that form from the water release holes.

Goo Gone is a great product for taking off unsightly sticky price labels on glass, plastic items, and it also removes hairspray. Read the label, as it is a very useful product. Apply Goo Gone to the sticky spot and let set a couple minutes, then wipe off. It will also take scuffmarks off linoleum and no-wax floors without damaging or dulling the surface. Always wipe off the floor with a regular cleaner afterward to avoid having a slick spot that someone could fall on. Clorox Clean-Up can also remove hairspray, if the surface won't be harmed by bleach.

Things Easily Forgotten

- Toilet paper holder
- Towel rack edges
- Windowsills
- Doorknobs and hinges
- Light switches
- Top of refrigerator
- Under cabinet edges
- Cobwebs
- Television screen
- Glass doors to television stand
- Inside microwave
- Top edge of shower stall
- Ceiling fans
- Behind doors
- Hutch top

If when leaving you realize you forgot to clean something that is very obvious, such as the front storm door, it would be wise to go back and do it. Use the spare rag and window cleaner you carry in your bag so as not to have to backtrack two more times through the house.

Before leaving the house, check to make sure you have *all* your belongings before shutting that door and being locked out. Did you remember your pay, purse, gloves, duster, kneeling pads, vacuum, equipment bag, cobweb chaser, and your car keys?

Spring Cleaning

What should I clean? You hire out to be a weekly cleaner; this doesn't involve spring-cleaning. You may want to clean very thorough the first couple times in a house. It may take you two or three times in a house to get it into good shape. Let them know this. One way to keep a job is to do some extras. They love it! Clean under their kitchen sink one day. You may never touch that spot again in months and your cleaning this area may inspire them to keep it spotless after that. Certain light fixtures may be very easy to clean, as access to them may be easy. Vary the extra things you do. It will keep them happy and keep you with a steady income!

Things NOT to clean unless by choice, trade-off, or paid extra

- Washing dishes
- Ironing
- Washing down walls
- Vacuuming down drapes
- Moving heavy furniture
- Cleaning screens
- Washing mini-blinds
- Cleaning silver
- Changing beds
- Cleaning upholstery
- Vacuuming spring /matress
- Flipping spring /matress
- Inside refrigerator
- Ceiling fixtures
- Inside range oven
- Linen closet
- Closets
- Inside fireplace and ashes
- Basement
- Garage
- Change cat litter box
- Removing shower doors
- Taking trash to treelawn
- Letting dog out
- Letting repairmen in
- Buying their products

Avoid cleaning basements. Basements the size of the whole structure can be quite time consuming to clean. It might have a room they use as a family room which can be just as detailed as an upstairs room. If you decide to agree to clean the extra area, make it worth your while. There might be times you will sweep a little into the garage, or shake the mat in front of the entrance door going into the utility room, to keep dirt from tracking in.

There will be certain persons that you will be more willing to clean and do extras things for, due to their health conditions. Someone on a walker, in a wheelchair, or an elderly person who doesn't have the strength to take out the garbage will certainly appreciate your doing this for them.

If they're in an apartment, they may want you to carry things down to a storage area in the basement for them, or perhaps wash a load of clothes while you're cleaning. It's nice to help out, if you can, but you should also be receiving reasonable compensation for your efforts. If you're cleaning a very small apartment and receiving $45, then it would be nice to help with some extras without charge.

Sunroom

A sunroom should not be considered as part of the main house when trying to establish your cleaning fee. Will this extra room be complicated or simple to clean?

Some houses will have a sunroom with windows or sliding glass doors all around the room. A quick dusting, wiping of tables with Windex, and vacuuming of the room may be very simple and part of your regular routine and all that is necessary to keep the client happy. If there are lots of plants as shown in the picture below, there will be many leaves and possibly dirt spills. Beware of any over-watering of plants. There may be wet areas on the carpeting that you will not want to vacuum over. Read the section on Equipment Upkeep on page 143 and 144.

It's the windows that will be time consuming to clean. They are usually considered as an extra that you would be paid for, or they may clean the windows themselves. When they want you to clean these windows, in and out, charge an extra ten dollars or more. This amount could vary depending on how many windows, or how difficult they are to clean. Are there lots of screens to remove and tracks to clean? Charge appropriately.

Chapter 6

Practical Advice

Time Saving Ideas

Some family members may still be in the house when you arrive to clean. Try to stay out of their way. Clean the downstairs first while they're upstairs using the bathroom and bedrooms. If the client likes to talk to you a little, be friendly and still continue to work as shown on the previous page. They will eventually see you need to keep up your pace and will leave you alone to work. If they leave in the middle of your cleaning, you might want to hold off vacuuming until they are gone so you don't have to repeat any work.

Carry a trash bag around to empty wastepaper baskets as you clean from room to room, or go to each room first and empty all of them at once. Choose the method that will save you time. It's nice when children are trained to empty all the baskets before garbage pick-up day, it lessens your load a little.

Clean wastepaper baskets with a disinfectant. Put extra clean bags in the bottom of the basket, and then put in the new fresh liner. Each time someone empties the full basket, the fresh new one is just taken from the bottom. This is very convenient for the householder and a time saver for you. Inform them of this so they don't dump them away by accident. Many professional business cleaners do this to save time.

If they have a cat or dog they will have pet hair clinging to the furniture and also on stairway carpeting. Pet hair can often be removed in globs with a wet scrub brush or a wet rubber glove. This method works on a lot of fabrics. If you do this with the glove on carpeted steps, be careful not to cut yourself on the carpet tacks at the edges.

Cleaning products:

Learn how to use cleaning products to your advantage. Experiment at home with new products, and with those your clients buy. Read the labels. A product may have many other uses. Product know how can help cut your amount of work time.

New cleaning products are continually coming on the market to help ease our burden. Watch in the stores and at trade shows for demonstrations of new cleaners, brushes, or mops. Make sure the products you choose will really help do the job.

To avoid carrying heavier bottles of cleaners in the caddy, put your ammonia and floor cleaning soap on a rag, put it in the

caddy, and mix it with water when ready to clean the floor. This would eliminate two heavy bottles of added weight and leave more room for other items. The rag with the cleaner might be enough to clean a small bathroom floor without using a bucket of water.

Carry a box of spare products in your car trunk, items that you can't clean without, just in case they didn't buy a product you really need. Especially the first time in a house, you don't want your pace slowed down trying to improvise. I suggest: Windex, polish, Lime-A-Way, Clorox Clean-Up, and ammonia.

Cold water rinse:

When rinsing soap down a sink, rinse with cold water. Rinsing with warm water takes longer, as the bubbles seem to multiply and don't go down the drain as quickly.

Rags:

Have more rags than usual your first time in to clean. If you're using their rags, carry extras in case you run out. Grab a clean rag for different things and you'll spend less time cleaning up streaks. Carry a bucket of clean rags around the house with you so you don't have to backtrack for them and waste time.

Telephone calls:

If they receive a lot of phone calls, don't answer their phone; it's time consuming and some of their calls may be business calls. Most people have answering machines or voice mail anyway. If they don't, you will find yourself having to run for a pencil and paper to write down messages.

Develop a routine:

When cleaning any house, it is good to have a routine doing the same order of work; you'll be less likely to forget certain things and it will save you time. Also, develop a routine in each room. Form good habits, so as not to have to backtrack and waste precious time.

It's best to clean the bathrooms first when you have the most energy. In the bathroom clean the toilet first, then the sink, mirror, tub, and the floor last. Develop the same habit in each bathroom. Dust and vacuum the bedrooms and half the house will be done.

When cleaning the bedrooms, usually all you need is the duster, polish, window cleaner, and rags. Keep the caddy by the doorway. Try hanging the Windex bottle off your left jean pocket while polishing the furniture. Try keeping the bottle with you at most times, as it is easy to misplace. Before vacuuming a room, give a quick glance back to see if you missed anything.

If you work as a team with another person, remind each other of various things to do. Don't assume the other person cleaned something. Perhaps they thought you did it. Work in separate rooms to solve this problem.

Safety Tips

Product safety:

Read product labels. Don't misuse products to avoid damaging articles or your health. Never mix together bleach, ammonia, or acid products. Mixing these together could form toxic fumes. Lime water desposit removers have an acid content. Window cleaners often have ammonia in them. Some cleansers, soap scum removers, and toilet bowl cleaners include bleach as one of their ingredients. Front labels usually show this addition of bleach as shown on the Soft Scrub bottle.

Ammonia can be mixed with certain floor cleaning products, such as Spic And Span. Read the labels on the bottles to be safe.

When there's a bleach tablet in the back of the toilet tank, don't use an acid type product to clean the toilet bowl.

If using a bleach tablet in the toilet tank, then it might be wise to use a bleach toilet bowl cleaner, which is compatible.

If you have problems with fumes in general, you may want to use some type of mask or a long folded diaper to cover your nose. Try not to breathe in a lot of ammonia fumes, especially when using it undiluted. Turn on a fan or open windows.

Work safely:

Never rush, running up and down stairways. Hold onto the railing when possible. Never try to carry too much up in one trip.

Set your caddy and bucket of rags just outside a small bathroom door, but always leave a pathway out of the room so you don't have to be stepping over things and trip.

When cleaning bathtubs or shower stalls, stand on a rag. It will prevent you from slipping, especially when the floor is already wet. Some products cause a slick film on the tub floor.

Many have razors setting around in tub areas and on shower stall seats. You may want to set these aside when you're cleaning to prevent yourself from falling on them and sustaining a serious cut.

If you wear tennis shoes that have worn tread on them, you're endangering yourself and increasing your chances of slipping and falling in showers and on wet floors. To assure safety, invest in a new pair of comfortable work shoes. Don't walk across wet floors with smooth soled shoes on.

Beware of standing on a toilet seat while cleaning. Many seats are flimsy and could suddenly break without warning.

It's much safer to work without rings on. Your fingers can get caught, especially when you're trying to move around fast. Harsh chemicals may harm the finish on your fine jewelry.

When using an upright vacuum, be careful when backing up not to bang your elbow into an opened door or glass hutch doors.

Be careful not to trip on the vacuum cord, try to keep it out of the way. Don't let the cord get into any puddles of water, and don't run over the cord. The rotator brushes could strip it to the bare wire. Check your cord periodically for bare wires, and wrap it with electrical tape until you can get it replaced.

Don't use a very wet rag when wiping outlets or light switches so you don't get shocked or start a fire. Never get a wet rag near an empty light bulb socket in a lamp or light fixture.

Many have electrical items plugged in near the bathroom sink; unplug these before working with water to avoid shock.

Only use a sturdy footstool or ladder. If it is shaky, have them buy another one. There are many two-step footstools. Find one that is sturdy and you are comfortable with.

When cleaning outside windows, beware of soft ground from rain or watering. Your ladder or stool legs could suddenly sink into the ground causing you to fall and perhaps injuring yourself.

NARROW STEPS
MIGHT BE HARDER
TO BALANCE ON

COSCO®
BIG STEP
(INDOOR USE ONLY)

MADE BY
RUBBERMAID®
(INDOOR USE ONLY)

Don't stand on the edge of a porcelain sink, it can break. You could get hurt and it would be very embarrassing to explain.

Never try to stand on a kitchen countertop in socks, which could cause you to slip and fall. Get a sturdy step stool or ladder for higher area work.

Unplug a toaster before using a wet cloth to avoid shock. Never, ever put a knife or fork down into a

toaster to remove a stuck piece of bread when it is still plugged in to the outlet, it can prove to be fatal.

Never stick your hand down a garbage disposal near the blades. If the switch is slightly out of place it can suddenly turn on.

Area rugs or homemade yarn rugs without proper backing can be very slippery on certain flooring. Suggest that they buy non-skid pads for under them to keep them from slipping. They can be cut to the size of the rug.

Keep doors locked while you're working and when no one else is there. You don't want any unsavory individuals walking in.

You are not obligated to let repairmen in the house to work when the client is gone. If they are expecting someone else, they will let you know and make arrangements with you ahead of time. Don't invite strangers into the house. Be careful who you open the door to.

Drink a lot of water while you're working or when you are hot in order to replace body fluids you lose through perspiration.

If you clean the hair out of a client's hairbrush that sets on a dresser, it would be good to wash your hands, because hair is full of germs.

If your client has a fire extinguisher, it might be good for you to read the directions and familiarize yourself on how to use it, in the event something happens while you are there.

Sometimes a client will have a gun in the house, perhaps under a matress, or as part of a gun collection. It would be best to just leave it alone and not touch. Let the owner take care of all firearms, whether on display or not!

Hand care:

Supply your own protective gloves, having an extra pair so as not to get caught without them when cleaning bathrooms. Using gloves protects you from not only bacteria but can keep you from getting certain skin conditions or rough, dry hands.

Never touch anyone else's blood with your bare hands on a job. None of us really know the health of other persons, so always use precautions in this regard. No one should leave blood smeared around for you to clean up. Wear gloves to clean up any blood, and use an antibacterial or disinfectant cleaner on that area. Be sure to wash your hands throughly.

When emptying wastebaskets, dump them into a large garbage bag instead of pulling things out by hand, to avoid getting cut with a razor, needle, or anything else sharp. You also don't want to be touching items thrown into a bathroom wastebasket, like dirty swabs and nose tissues. You could very easily catch a cold from touching a dirty tissue. You might want to have your gloves on for this task.

If people are home ill in the house, wash your hands a lot and don't be touching your face. Use antibacterial products on any areas that are commonly touched by hands: light switches, handles, doorknobs, and countertops.

Some clients will have their hot water tanks on a high heat setting. The hot water is great for soaking range burner trays, but be careful not to get burned. Use your rubber gloves or add cold water to eliminate a sink full of hot water.

If you get a burn from a range burner, iron, or hot curling iron, swiftly get to a faucet and run cold water over the burnt area for a couple minutes. This will reduce the burn damage and lessen later pain.

Wash your hands often, especially after cleaning bathrooms. When you have finished cleaning the bathroom, wash your hands, and then dry the sink to a shine. Before you leave the job, wash in the utility tub so you don't splatter a sink you have already cleaned. Wash your hands thoroughly to give the soap time to kill the germs. Use their antibacterial hand soap if available. It's more sanitary to use liquid soap from a dispenser than using a bar of soap that everyone touches, especially in public restrooms. When bars of soap are used much of the dirt from a

person's hand stays on the bar, so it needs to be rinsed after it's been used so it will be clean for the next user. After washing, rinse your hands well so the germs eliminate down the drain with the water.

After using a toilet, never walk away without washing your hands. This is safer for you and keeps you from spreading germs around for others to pick up from touching dirty doorknobs, railings, etc. Everyone, whether at home or in a public place, should always wash their hands.

Never put your hands down into a garbage disposal and always have your gloves on for toilet cleaning.

You could also keep a small bottle of hand sanitizer in your car, in case you leave and have forgotten to wash your hands. This product is very useful for emergencies. If you forgot to wash your hands, don't touch your mouth or eyes, or shake hands with someone else. Go wash your hands with soap and water as soon as possible.

If you have any cuts or open sores on your hands, cover with plastic bandage strips that resist coming off in water. Wear rubber gloves to help the bandage to stay on longer.

Clean your fingernails using a metal file to eliminate germs.

You might want to use a good hand lotion to keep your hands from drying out, especially more so in the winter months or when you have used a lot of ammonia and harsher chemicals to strip floors. Wear gloves if you have skin reactions to cleansers, or if you tend to get eczema on your hands.

Always wear something on your fee, such as shoes, or slippers, or socks when working to protect your feet from injury. Do not work barefoot!

Exiting the house:

If you need to exit the house through the garage door, carry your equipment out first, then come back to push the automatic garage door opener, so as not to delay getting out and under before the garage door comes down. Exit swiftly. Some people may worry that the door will come down and hit you. Others will have a code box on the outside of the garage door. They may give you the number to punch in, so you can enter the house through the garage instead of giving you a key.

Some garage doors now have safety devices installed, which prevent you from leaving that way. If you run out under the door when it's coming down, it will automatically go back up. The client will have to arrange another way for you to exit and still have the house locked up. Some people find it easier to give you a key.

Protect your back:

Learn to protect you back. Pick up items closer to your body, not with outstretched arms. Bend your legs at the knees to pick up something heavier off the floor.

Don't be moving very heavy furniture without help on your cleaning jobs. A queen size sofa sleeper can be extremely heavy and something you shouldn't have to move on a cleaning job. This type of task could be considered a part of the client's spring cleaning project for themselves.

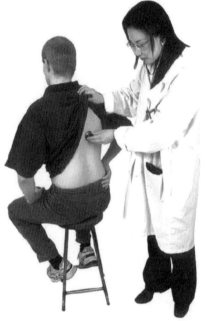

Pick up a vacuum turned backwards and leaning against your hip using some leverage, if convenient. Some vacuums will have a special handle to make it easy for you to pick it up. Vacuum handles will vary with the different brands, as well as the weight. Vacuums with power drive are often more heavy. Roll the vacuum on its wheels when taking it into a house, unless the sidewalk is dirty. This will help save your back, but will wear out any plastic wheels quicker than usual.

Be careful when you're on a ladder. Don't bend back too far and lose your balance, or don't hold a bent position too long and strain your back. Many people today suffer from back problems, so try not to strain your back.

Don't walk across wet floors if you don't have to. Clean the direction so you can exit out of the room without walking across the wet floor. Don't spray furniture polish on a floor. It would make it very slippery and someone could fall and get hurt.

Be careful walking up to their house in the snow or on ice. If they don't use ice melt or rock salt, you could easily slip.

On the first day of your cleaning a client's house, you may be taking in things you wouldn't ordinarily. Don't carry too many supplies into a house all at once. Make a couple trips into the house, otherwise, you might strain your back.

Heavy garbage bags should be left for the householder to dispose of. Don't strain your back with too much trash in one bag. You don't necessarily have to stuff a bag to the top.

Be careful how you pick up your vacuum to put it into the car trunk. Grab the vacuum with one hand at each end.

You may aggravate a bad back when using an upright vacuum on a stairway. If you already have back problems, you will have to be more careful. Perhaps the client has an electric hand vacuum you can use instead.

If you are stripping a kitchen floor that day, it may be too difficult to clean other rooms without over-tiring your back.

If your back is hurting, you can slow down your pace of work, or put off some of the harder work until your next visit. You could also take a short break.

If you injure your back on the job, you may not have the pain until a day or two later. Back pain often occurs later. As a result of this, it can be hard to determine just what caused the problem.

Protect your knees:

Many people now have ceramic tile floors and other hard surfaces that you will have to kneel on. Make sure you use some type of kneeling pads if you plan on cleaning houses regularly, otherwise, you'll likely develop knee problems as time goes on. Refer back to pages 36 and 37 for more information on the advantages of the different types of pads and instructions on how to assemble and sew your own.

Do's and Don'ts

Leave your home at a reasonable time to allow for unexpected hindrances, such as trains, detours, or traffic jams. Try your best not to be late to your job.

Don't eat their food and drink, unless they have specifically offered. It's best to bring your own quick snack, if needed.

If you perspire heavily, stop to wipe off or wear a sweat headband to prevent dripping on furniture. Drink plenty of water while working to replenish your body fluids.

There are many people that don't want anyone smoking in their home. You are there to work, and it is more efficient to be

working with both hands and not having something else to slow you down. The client won't want ashes being dropped on their flooring. If you have to smoke, step out into the garage or outside. Make sure you don't lock yourself out of the house, it would cause a lot of inconvenience for everyone.

Make sure your shoe soles are clean when wearing them in the client's house. If you wear tennis shoes to work in, check the tread regularly for any dirt lodged in the cracks. Clean them with a brush, soap and water, rinse the sole without wetting the rest of the shoe. Dry the soles with a rag.

Wear shoes, socks, or slippers when cleaning. Some people could be quite annoyed if you walked on their floors barefoot. Most people don't mind if you wear shoes because you're less likely to injure your feet or break a toe. Have shoes on when cleaning a shower stall to prevent falling or getting wet socks.

If you break something, glue it together and inform them of what happened. They will appreciate your honesty and will most likely not be upset anyway. You are the one that will suffer the most, worrying about how they will react.

Turn the vacuum off if the client answers the phone in the same room. If they have a portable phone, they will likely move to another area. If not, try to do something else in the meantime.

Don't tell other people about the private lives of the clients.

If you answer the phone at their house, don't tell strangers their business or where they are. Just tell them to call back later, or to call back and leave a message on their answering machine. It's better to let their machine or voice mail pick up their messages. Some people receive a lot of calls due to their line of work.

Wear a watch that is easy to see and water resistant. Usually the larger round faced watches are more water resistant; delicate watches might fog up under the crystal. Check the time about halfway through the job, to keep yourself at a certain pace to be able to complete all projects in a set time.

Don't forget to take your pay they left for you. If they leave it on the kitchen table, put it in your wallet when you clean the kitchen. Once you pull the door shut to leave, you may be locked out if you don't have their key or a garage code. It can be time consuming to make a trip back to their house for your pay.

Replug anything you removed such as a lamp or toaster.

Don't unplug coffeepots or other appliances that have clocks on them. It would mess up the time.

Turn off the radio or television, if you were listening to either while you were working.

If you changed the thermostat, be sure to put it back where they had it set. If you think you'll forget, write yourself a note. It would be better not to be changing it to begin with.

Don't unplug any light timers, as they're usually set to come on at a certain time. These are often used when on vacation.

Try to keep a pen and a small notebook with you. You'll be leaving them notes with lists of products they need to buy. If they leave you a tip, be sure to take the time to write a thank you note.

Turn off all the lights before you exit, unless they request otherwise.

Lock all doors when you leave or whatever they have instructed you to do.

If you're the homeowner and your house cleaner neglected a certain item, ask the cleaner to clean this object today. Just mentioning this will remind the person to give this regular attention without a complaint.

Equipment Upkeep

Vacuum:

Regular upkeep of your own vacuum cleaner that you take on jobs is necessary. Make sure you clean the bottom brushes and wipe off the bottom plate that covers around the brush assembly with clear ammonia on a rag, as shown in the picture. You may need to do this every week or two. If you're cleaning  several homes a week, this upkeep will help keep the client's carpeting cleaner.

Never vacuum when the brushes are wet. It could make dirt brush marks on the carpet, and then you would have to spend time cleaning that off. Do spot clean-up on carpet with clear ammonia when necessary.

Vacuum belts stretch after a period of time and need to be replaced periodically for proper dirt pick up. When a belt is stretched out, the roller will not be making the correct amount of revolutions and therefore, will not be picking up properly. If the edge of a throw rug got caught in the brush assembly, the belt probably stretched out. Compare the old belt to the new one when you change it, to see the difference in size.

A power driven vacuum will have two belts, one for the rotating brush and a smaller belt to make the vacuum move. A stretched power drive belt will make the vacuum harder to move, and will not pick up dirt as well. A belt can also pop off its roller and will suddenly stop pulling the vacuum that is power driven. Learn how to put these belts on so you don't get caught without a usable vacuum. When changing vacuum belts, do so over linoleum or a washable floor. Often little black particles fall out from a belt that is slightly chewed up from being askew.

Check the cord for bare wires and wrap with electrical tape until you can get the cord replaced. Never let the cord with bare wires get into a puddle of water.

Change the dirt bag before it becomes overly stuffed. The vacuum will pick up better and carry fewer odors. Vacuums that have dirt bags where the dirt falls in from the upper part of the bag work so much better than the type that push up from the bottom.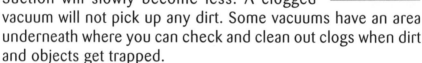

Never vacuum up any water or a spot of wet carpeting. The moisture could go inside the vacuum and dirt will stick to the internal parts and clog the fan, causing future problems. Suction will slowly become less. A clogged vacuum will not pick up any dirt. Some vacuums have an area underneath where you can check and clean out clogs when dirt and objects get trapped.

A vacuum that is stored in the trunk of a car when it is freezing weather outside may not perform as well as expected until it gets warmed up. The belts will not work as smoothly and the vacuum may make strange noises, and the belts may wobble and want to fall off their rollers. Place it over a heat register to warm it up to eliminate the problem.

If you have to carry your vacuum out through the snow in the winter, don't set it down unless the brush area is covered. Snow can get caught in the brushes. If the brushes do get wet, set it by a register in the house.

When you find it hard to unwind a vacuum cord, wind the cord looser when putting it away and it will be easier to take off the next usage. Some models have the top handle you wrap around that swings down to remove the cord with ease. Turn it back up to rewind when finished vacuuming.

There may be a hook on the top of the handle where you can attach the cord so it doesn't get in your way while vacuuming. It helps to keep from running over the cord and getting it caught in the rotating brush. Some vacuums are so powerful that when the cord gets caught it will scrape the rubber off down to the bare wires.

Some clients may insist you use their vacuum to avoid your vacuum from bringing in fleas from someone else's house. They may ask if any of your other clients have pets. If you think a client's cat or dog has fleas, use their vacuum instead of yours to protect your other jobs.

Dusters:

Long-handled nylon dusters work well on some items, but don't use them around a hot light bulb; you'll get a quick meltdown. Shake the dusters regularly close to the floor to avoid dust floating through the air and back onto the furniture. Some dusters can be washed by hand and spun in the dryer. Set outside to dry or fluff a little in the clothes dryer. Whether it's lambs wool, nylon, or yarn, they need to be cleaned. A dust cloth should also be thrown in with the rags to be washed every time it is used.

If you use Old English Scratch Cover or Liquid Gold, throw the rag away or store it in a sealed plastic bag for use another time. Never wash it with the other rags, the oil or odors could spread to the others.

Caddy:

Keep the caddy clean. When you've finished cleaning the house, it would be good to rinse out the caddy, dry it, and put it away. Some people will store their products right in the caddy, others will keep them on shelves when not in use. Make sure all chemicals have the lids tightened to avoid spills. Put the Clorox Clean-Up bottle in the off position to avoid accidents.

Brushes:

It's a good habit to rinse out brushes right after you use them, especially if you used a bleach product. This will prevent you from ruining something else. Tap the toilet bowl edge three or four times with the toilet bowl brush to eliminate excess water from the brush before storing it away. Empty water out of the brush holder and clean occasionally.

Scents:

There are scented flakes that can be tossed on the floor and vacuumed up to deodorize the inside dirt bag. One caution with this is that many people are now allergic to many fragrances. Vacuum repair shops sometimes add scents to the bag.

Never sprinkle powdery type carpet deodorizers that might sink into the carpet that would cause clogging in the vacuum or gum up the carpet. Some use them to cover pet odors. If they insist on using these products, use their vacuum. If you're not sure about a product, ask your vacuum repairman.

Rubber or vinyl gloves:

Heavier gloves can be washed to keep clean and avoid musty smells. The outside can be washed easily by washing your hands with the gloves still on. Wash the gloves in warm soap water, rinse well, and hang up to dry or toss in the dryer for a couple minutes. You could turn them inside out to dry, then reverse.

Sponge mop:

Don't run a sponge mop over a floor register or concrete. It will cause the sponge to crumble. Rough edged ceramic grout will ruin the sponge quickly too.

Never wipe up a bleach product with the mop; it will eat away at the sponge.

When you are finished with the sponge mop, rinse it off with clean water first before putting it away. Squeeze out any excess water to speed up drying. Store in an upright position to protect the sponge or perhaps they have an area where it can be hung. If the sponge leans against the wall, it will leave a dirty spot or even harm the paint. The Sponge Squeezer on the Magic Mop is suppose to remain wet when not in use.

Cobweb chaser:

A cobweb chaser should be hung or leaned in such a way to prevent the bristles from being smashed. You can knock a lot of dust off the Webster by running your hand across the bristles. They may also be washed and set out in the sun to dry.

Record Your Earnings

Keep good records of your income in a notebook or cash journal as shown below. Record the name, date and amount earned from each client. You are required by law to pay federal income tax on this income. Also check your state and local government for any requirements.

Record any expenses related to your business for income tax deductions. For instance, you can deduct the following items: sweeper cost, bags, belts, repairs, brushes, rags, buckets, brooms, mops, chemicals, cobweb chaser, car expenses and insurance, gas receipts, mileage notes, advertising fees, calendar, business cards, address book, record book, flyer copies, and any work related insurance or bonding fees.

Business Insurance

These are optional insurance plans that occasionally someone cleaning may desire or need for their business.

Insurance:

As a cleaner, there is insurance available to cover anything you or your employees might be liable for at a client's house. This would include breakage of items, injury to an animal, or other things that could cause you to be liable. This cost for an individual policy could be about $350 a year for a million dollar coverage. This fee would increase as payroll increases from hiring employees should you decide to expand your business.

Bonded:

This is an insurance guarantee against theft. The client's claim would be paid, and then the insurer collects this amount from you, the insured. The cost would be about $100 a year for $5,000 coverage.

Index

About the Author

Carol J. Klima, a professional housecleaner for more than 23 years, has put her expertise in print to help other people cope with their busy lives. She resides in North Ridgeville, Ohio with her husband, a retired sheet metal worker. The couple have two children and 7 grandchildren. Carol enjoys sitting down to a good novel for relaxation and country line dancing for activity.

She frequently speaks concerning the care of aging parents for groups and trade shows, including being featured on HGTV's show "Dream Builders." Carol has always been an organizer, which has led her to becoming an author through experience of designing in-law suite floor plans and writing the book: *"Build Your Own In-Law Suite - Floor Plans and More."*

Letters from readers

I would love to receive your comments of how this publication helped you. If you have a personal funny experience related to housecleaning, please share this with me. Send letters to:

Carol Klima
c/o Homestead Press
8804 Harris Ct.
North Ridgeville, OH 44039